Eternal Memory

by
Ann Walko

Sterling House

Pittsburgh, PA

ISBN 1-56315-167-7

Paperback Fiction
© Copyright 1999 Ann Walko
All rights reserved
First Printing—1999
Library of Congress #98-87120

Request for information should be addressed to:

SterlingHouse Publisher, Inc.
The Sterling Building
440 Friday Road
Pittsburgh, PA 15209
www.sterlinghousepublisher.com

Cover design: Michelle Vennare - SterlingHouse
Typesetting: Drawing Board Studios
Cover art: The Seamstress, by Cara, an original painting from the
private collection of Thomas S. Sterling

Printed in Canada

When he established the heavens I was there,
when he marked out the vault over the face of the deep;
When he made firm the skies above,
when he fixed fast the foundations of the earth,
I was beside him.

Prov. 8: 27-30

Acknowledgments

Harry J. Mooney, Professor, Department of English, University of Pittsburgh, for reading every beginning page I had given him, for the many, many corrections, for as many nice comments, and, especially, for words like "excellent," strewn throughout.

Edna Machesney, President of The Pittsburgh Poetry Society, for continued and unfailing support.

JoAnn Richard, for the mountains of typing and retyping.

Ed Wintermantel, *The Pittsburgh Press*, for publishing my first stories.

Friends, Marian Begala, Joan Huber, Polly Silliman and Phyllis Lewis for continued and never failing support.

Lee Shore Agency and SterlingHouse Publisher for taking me on and for providing absolutely super editing.

And finally, my husband, John, for making sure, once I sat down to the typewriter, that nothing interrupted me.

WHO'S WHO:

On Pap's Side:
Aunt Julie, Pap's oldest sister
Uncle Maksim, her husband
Uncle George, Pap's older brother. Wife and children still in Europe.

On Mama's Side:
Uncle Mike, Mama's oldest brother;
Wife and children still in Europe.
Aunt Liza, Mama's first cousin
Uncle Jakub, her husband

Gavaj, permanent boarder. Wife and children in Europe.

Actual people, same name:
Pap
Mama
Uncle George
Gavaj
Miss Mellon
Mr. Gilchrist
Mr. Silianoff
The Murrays
The Simmons
School friends
The people that came

Actual people, different name:
Aunt Julie, Uncle Maksim and Little Julie
Aunt Liza, Uncle Jakub and Little Liza
The Donelkos
Susie
Uncle Fedor
Ilonka

Events:
All took place. Some shifted in time.

Table of Contents

PART III

Introduction

My stories are about a people who came from the foothills of the Carpathian Mountains, the *Pod Karpacki Rus*, named by the Greeks, the Ruthenians.

Not much has been said about the people of whom I write. Living undisturbed in the shadow of the Tatra Mountain, the historian passed them by. I will share an observation made in the early 1930s.

Unrest in Central Europe prompted *LIFE* magazine to do an article about the area. Included was a map of the region. At once my attention was centered on the spot from whence my people came. There was *Kosice*, then, to the east, the smaller-lettered *Mihalovce*, where I began to read: "the least civilized people of Europe live here." Least civilized? Of all Europe? Mentally I hugged the phrase. What did *LIFE* know?

When America opened its doors — when a thoroughfare was forged from there to here, they came, and that which missed the grasp of the chronicler, came with them. Pockets of Slavic peoples sprang up all over the new land; wherever there was a need for labor, they settled, a sauerkraut barrel in every cellar, a slab of bacon on every table, and strings of mushrooms drying at the back of every stove.

Many years ago, Walter Cronkite said of the early immigration period:

> ". . . in the history of mankind this never happened
> before, and will never happen again."

This is not only true of the period—it is also true of the Slavic peasant who came to these shores at the time: It will never happen again.

———————

Prologue

*". . . rest the soul of Thy servant where there is neither
pain nor sorrow, but life everlasting . . . ."*
(From the Byzantine Prayer for the Dead)

ALL SOULS' DAY

It was All Souls' Day, and I was on my way to Church, and already the present was beginning to blend into the past. As it is now, so it was in the beginning: A misty fog over-layered the landscape, blending trees into hillside — first a mist, then the trees, then running, scampering creatures, and I, already there, a hominid, adapting, stumbling, remembering.

And now wondering. *Was it frightening, little Hominid? You must have had fun with the little creatures, but the big ones? Were you afraid? You must have been. But you made it. If you hadn't, I would not be here. But you made it. And so will I. Thanks, little Hominid. Thanks. When I get to church I'll light a candle for you.*

As I neared the church, I noticed the stooped black-clad figure of Mrs. Donelko making her way stolidly, stubbornly across the street. I hurried to help her, hoping she would look up and see me coming, but, of course, she didn't dare. The imps that flit in and out of the paths of the elderly would surely have tripped her. When I reached her side, she was already near the curb. I touched her arm.

"Hanicka!" she cried, calling me by the diminutive.

I caught her arm, greeted her in the Slavonic, *"Slava Isusu Christu."*

"Slava na viki" she replied, leaning on my arm, looking at me. The light in her eyes wavered, then held, shining with the joy of being remembered — at being lifted once more out of the shroud that was, even as we stood there, beginning to enfold her.

"Slava I na viki," she breathed again as we made our way through the church door.

The interior of the church was dimly lit by a small vigil lamp before the altar and the flickering of a few All Souls' Day candles from the votive stands. The ladies were already assembled for Rosary.

"Waiting, the dear ladies, for me," whispered Mrs. Donelko. But first we had to light our candles.

As we walked toward the candles, I glanced along the pews, at the shadowy faces somberly fixed on the lone altar light, heads nodding in fervent communication with a favorite saint, or, if the plea be desperate, the Blessed Mother.

At the stand, Mrs. Donelko murmured, to herself, "Seven." I gave her a lighted taper, then took a light from her. First Grandma, then Pap, Mama, two little sisters, one little brother, aunts, uncles, a block across the top for each of the boarders, then waited for Mrs. Donelko to finish, then remembered: *Little Hominid, I almost forgot you.* I found a perfect candle at the top. There. Then back to the pews, Mrs. Donelko to join the ladies and I, to my accustomed place, across from them. Despite the shifting of all eyes toward the two of us, the progression of the beads and the movement of lips didn't even falter.

Over on the men's side and a little to the front of the ladies was Sirochman, another one of the old ones. He never missed a prayer session, and not because of a desire to pray. He liked teasing the ladies.

"The interminable praying. How weary God must be to listen to so much. And the confessing? What could they possibly confess? The priest has to be tired of listening. And all those trips to the altar. All his wine you drink up."

His attack on *Soshi Sickuri* (Social Security) was a few notches above just teasing. "Time was," he would say, "if a man lost a wife, his friends would quickly find him another 'good yet' woman who had just lost a husband. Now the *babi* have become *indipendee:* fold their hands over their ample stomachs and wait for the next check to come in. No one to make an old man a cup of tea as God commanded; no one to warm his bed at night as God ordained." The smile on the face of each lady took on a pensive look; there was a comfort in the old way that the new did not provide.

Despite the banter, it was he who led the rosary, enjoying to the hilt the role of being the only man present. He was now clearing his throat, rising from his knees, a signal to the ladies that he was about to begin. "Straight as a candle yet," he would brag. In a sure voice, he gave the introduction, then back to his knees.

As in one voice, the group began the five decades of the Sorrowful Mysteries, rising and falling in a mesmeric chant that had the effect of pushing aside the veil that separated the living from the dead.

The church began to fill up, the lighted candles multiplied. Each votive stand began to represent a congregation of its own. "Hail Mary, full of grace . . . pray for us . . . now and at the hour . . . Amen."

At completion of the rosary, Sirochman, "straight as a candle yet," rose from his knees. Time for the concluding prayer. Time for Mass to begin.

This was also the cue for the altar boys to begin lighting the candles on the altar. Some lights flared quickly, eagerly grasping for life, others just as adamantly refusing. I began to wonder: *Who were the souls so resentful of the call back to Earth?*

One candle especially was giving the altar boy an inordinate amount of trouble. Again and again he tried, borrowing from an adjoining unflinching flare but to no avail. *Who could that be? Uncle Maksim? Refusing a light from Aunt Julie? Is that how it was? Whatever had been would be continued in the hereafter? Forever? Is that why we are here praying for them?*

Poor Aunt Julie. How unkind all of us had been. For the first time in my life I was heartily sorry for having offended her so many times. *Please, Uncle Maksim, take the light.* After what seemed forever, the light took hold, flared, began to burn. *Thank you, God.*

A light, dipping up and down as if playing an instrument, caught my eye. Uncle Fedor. Another was leaning over to one side, stubbornly alive. Who else but Mr. Donelko? It's payday night. He is weaving his way home from a local tavern. And making it. And the one next to him, glowing brightly, now of itself, now taking its sparkle from the others, was Susie. I can still hear her. "Can I come with you, Annie? Can I?" And I yelling back, "No, you can't. I have to hurry. Mama said for me to hurry." Did I have to?

My eyes, now filled with tears, looked beyond the altar at the window of the Blessed Mother, at the colors: the reds, the yellows, the blues. The colors began to blend, then into a separate remembered pattern. It was Mama's apron. She was sitting in her rocker holding the baby and I was leaning against her, tracing the colors of her apron, now red, now yellow, now blue, and listening. She was telling us a story.

Part I

First there was a Wedding

And when the wedding was over, mama was saying, "I was already the mistress of a house — this house — complete with boarders. Eight of them. On my first morning, at this very table, I counted nine buckets — the ninth, your father's — all in a row, all looking at me, all seeming to be saying, 'We're waitin'.'"

"What did you do?"

"Do? If Uncle Mike hadn't guided me through that first morning, I don't know what I would have done."

Here, kind reader, I must interject. Mama, we learned later, had slept all night behind the door on her own *perina* (feather tick), not unusual being that marriages were usually arranged, the bride and groom often never having seen each other until the visit to the priest. Mama's story continues:

"When I came into the kitchen, Uncle Mike and your father already had the fire going and the coffee pot on. Pork pieces were sizzling in the oven and the bread was on the table ready for slicing.

"We began with the lunch buckets. These came in two parts. Into the bottom, well sugared and creamed with canned milk, went the coffee. Yes, directly into the pail. Into the top section went the rest of the lunch, and there is yet no better way to make a sandwich. A slice of bread was dipped into the nicely browned pork fat, spread with mustard, topped with a piece of pork, then covered with another slice of bread. Another sandwich was made with butter and jelly, then both wrapped in a small *chlebovka* — a napkin.

"And always, a piece of fruit. When the boarders came down for breakfast, the lunch buckets were already packed, standing in a row on the sideboard.

"Like soldiers, ready for war,' Uncle Mike used to say.

"For breakfast, the men had the rest of the pork, bread slathered with mustard and the ever-present coffee. In the Old Country, coffee was so rare it was given only to pregnant women."

We never tired of hearing the story of Mama's first days in this country. She arrived on a Friday, met Pap that evening. Saturday morning, accompanied by Aunt Julie, the two went to the parish house. Beginning that Sunday, then on the following two Sundays, banns were read. Four weeks from the day Mama stepped off the boat, the wedding took place.

"What did you wear?" we asked.

"Wear? A white dress. Borrowed. Aunt Julie made the veil, and we borrowed the rings."

"Borrowed?"

Mama shrugged her shoulders, as if to say: That's how it was.

"But there was plenty to eat. Aunt Julie did the cooking and the baking. Uncle Mike took care of the drinks, and Pap and I went around to let the people know. No written invitations in those days. The people would have been insulted.

"The wedding was in Aunt Julie's house. One room was emptied: first to eat in, cleared to dance in, then again, set to eat in, then to dance in. A gypsy band from Braddock played from morning until night. And when the wedding was over, after we had cleaned up, put the furniture back into place, your father and I came here, to this house, already full of boarders."

"Who took care of them before you got here?"

"Another family lived here. The Marcins. Before that, it was Uncle Mike and Aunt Mary, but Aunt Mary wanted to go back. Uncle Mike stayed here.

"When the Marcins decided on going back — many people did that in those days — Uncle Mike thought of me. Time for me to marry. Time to come to America.

"Working with Uncle Mike was a young man waiting for the right girl to come, and when he learned that the young man came from the very next village, the marriage was arranged."

"Were you excited?"

"Excited? I was scared. I didn't want to get married. But I did want to come to America. 'It will be good for you,' wrote Uncle Mike. I came. But when I saw Pap, I was disappointed."

Disappointed? How could she say that?

Seeing the disbelief in my face, she added, and her voice hugged the sounds of laughter, "He didn't like me either. If I could have, I would have swum back to the Old Country."

"Mama! What would we have done?"

But, as Mama often said, that was no time for foolishness. She was whirled at once into the maelstrom that was the New Country: the men off to work, women to theirs. "All clothing had to be soaked, then rubbed, then boiled in a huge copper boiler, rinsed in bluing water, starched, then hung out to dry. Pap had the lines stretched before he went to work. When winter came, the clothes were hung in the attic.

"Ironing was done with an iron heated on the stove top, then clicked into a handle."

Mama, as did all newcomers, followed a weekly pattern already established by earlier immigrants, already immortalized in a nursery rhyme:

> This is the way we wash our clothes,
> wash our clothes,
> wash our clothes;
> This is the way we wash our clothes,
> Early on Monday morning.

The nursery rhyme held true, but it didn't tell everything — it didn't tell that first the water had to be pumped and carried into the kitchen, that the copper boiler, already on the fired-up stove, had to be filled, then the tubs.

It didn't tell that first the clothes, beginning with the "whites," had to be soaked, wrung by hand, then thrown into another tub to be rubbed with naphtha soap on a washboard, wrung out, thrown into the boiler with more naphtha, to boil.

Waiting for the clothes to come to a boil, the rest of the laundry was prepared, ending with men's work clothes.

After boiling, the clothes were lifted out with a broom handle into a tub for a final rubbing, then wrung into first one rinse water, then another with bluing in it, then, finally, out to dry — a beautiful sight on a breezy, sunny day, each lady vying to be the first with her laundry out. Some cheated: A few pieces on the line before her work had begun — a minor fault, considering that the highest compliment to a woman was to say she's up before dawn.

Tuesday was for ironing, and again, not the way the nursery rhyme put it. All pieces were starched, dampened, rolled up. Irons were heated on the stove top, and when hot enough, tested by the tip of a wet finger, carried to the ironing board, and as the iron cooled, another was waiting on the stove.

In rhythmic order, the week continued: Mending on Wednesday, shopping on Thursday, Friday baking, and scrubbing on Saturday, then all together to church on Sunday to honor and worship the Great Creator Who started it all: Who, after separating the earth from the land, brought forth the sun to warm each stirring creature, to awaken, both male and female, each to his appointed task — through the long centuries, never deviating, never questioning — to nudge, cajole, each sleepy head into another day: Pap and the men to work, to a job, and Mama, at once, to the chores of the day: to clean, to cook, to nourish.

And, following the established pattern, before a year was up, a little girl was born to them.

Maybe it was the hustle and the bustle of the period: So many changes, so many adjustments, so many babies — every Sunday a christening somewhere that maybe even God couldn't keep up. When Merka came, she wasn't properly formed.

Maybe that is why in a few months God took her back. But He didn't forget them. Before another year was up, He gave them another little girl. Me.

Our Boarders

There were many households such as ours. Wherever there was a need for laborers, be it the steel mills of Braddock and Homestead, the coal mines of Clymer, Pennsylvania, or the railroads that crisscrossed this country, there were nice little pockets of Old Country.

We lived in a four-room house that faced the vast Pitcairn Railroad Yards. Downstaris was a large kitchen with steps that led to the cellar, a back bedroom for us, then a hallway with steps that led to the upstairs two room. The upstairs bedrooms nicely accommodated eight men: two beds to a room, two men to a bed. In the attic were two cots for transients who came looking for work. Because of night shifts, some of the beds were occupied both night and day.

In addition to the beds, each room had a small table with a kerosene lamp, a closet, a chair. When winter came, a small coal stove provided a cheerful place for the men to sit around while waiting for supper call. Near each stove was a spittoon. On each wall was an icon for praying and over the door a cross, touched by each occupant as he left the room. And trunks.

Each boarder had his own trunk in which he kept all his belongings, a condition that not only kept the rooms neat and tidy, but provided the owner with a needed sense of privacy.

The trunks, fascinating objects of whorls and shining brass with steel bands all around, also told much of the character of their owners. Some were solidly built along massive lines, some had nice rounded tops, others just ordinary square shapes. They kept their places, primly, proudly, or, as in the case of a small, battered thing, even pensively, until the owner returned from work. Once opened, each trunk seemed to come alive, each complementing its owner. Oddments of personal items nestled in cubicles lined with designs of every hue. There was no limit to the variety. The delicate colors must have been a balm to a man yearning for the green fields of his village. Yes, the designs were flowers and trees, but the pungent smell rising from the opened trunks was tobacco; it pervaded every single thing inside.

The contents of each trunk consisted of simple necessary articles for a simple necessary existence. The large bottom section held mostly clothing: an extra shirt, long underwear, socks, pieces of leather for shoes, and — neatly wrapped in a piece of cloth — Sunday shoes.

The top compartment was much more interesting. Divided into small sections, it held letters from the Old Country, needles, pins, buttons and thread, some shoe polish, a shaving mug and a razor with a honing strop. And no matter how well you managed to hide the strop, it was found.

Uncle Fedor had a kewpie doll he won at a circus, and Gavaj had a book full of beautiful hymns, and a psalter from which he read when somebody died. He also had pen and ink for writing letters, and if you wanted to write, to see if you could because it looked so easy, you had to be careful and not spill the ink because it would never wash out and you'd never be allowed upstairs again.

Even if he couldn't read, each man had a prayer book to carry to church, the important places marked with a holy picture, and if you didn't put the picture back exactly the way you found it, somebody in church would have to turn the book right side up again and you got scolded. How did they know it was I?

One more thing: Down in one of the hidden corners lived a little green man, and if you just peeked into a trunk, he would leap out and grab you, and that was the truth. If you pressed your ear against the trunk and kept very still, you could hear him breathing. Once I tried to sneak some chewing gum out of Uncle Fedor's trunk and he squeaked at me. I dropped the lid. Anyhow, his chewing gum always tasted like tobacco.

Everything tasted like tobacco. And smelled like tobacco because all they did was sit around and smoke their pipes. Smoke and talk. I can still smell the tobacco. And if I close my eyes, I can still hear their voices.

I like to go back to the sounds that broke the early morning hours: Mama in the kitchen shaking down the ashes in the stove. Pap carrying them out. Mama building a fire and Pap bringing in the water, slamming the door hard against the wintry wind, and I in the back bedroom, snuggled close to Mary and Mikie under a huge feather tick.

I remember the sizzling sound of roasting pieces of pork punctuated by the timpani sound of lunch buckets being prepared, and all the while, in counterpoint, the halting, grumbling sounds of the men upstairs, yawning, coughing, grunting, for all the world like sleepy bull fiddles reluctantly roused for the morning litany.

As they dressed, each mumbled his prayers, then, one at a time, still in prayer, clunked heavily down the stairs. As they passed our bedroom door, I could hear one, then another finishing, "In the name of the Father, the Son, and the Holy Spirit, Amen," because, already from the kitchen, came the smell of food.

Breakfast was always the same: roast pork pieces, homemade bread, stewed prunes and coffee.

After breakfast, each man picked up his own lunch bucket, and with an exchange of "God give you a good day," they left for work: to the Roundhouse, where great steam engines were washed and watered; to the Transfer Yards where merchandise was re-loaded onto either the East or the Westbound humps where new freight trains were made up; or to road gangs where new tracks were laid or old ones repaired. How thankful they were for work to do, and how envious if one had an easier or cleaner job than the other. But no matter, when evening brought them home again, each entered the house with a "Praised God," to which Mama would answer, "Praised be forever."

The men took turns washing up: summertime out on the back porch, and wintertime at the bench behind the kitchen door.

After washing, all went upstairs until the call for supper. Sometimes there was a letter from the Old Country. And always a newspaper. Gavaj subscribed to all Slavic papers. Some of the men could read a little but Gavaj was the only one who could read and write. He could even read handwriting.

Meantime, Pap was helping Mama, and as soon as the table was set, I took my place at the upstairs doorway waiting for a signal to call the men to supper.

How I reveled in my position: those invitingly increasing sounds that tumbled down the stairs, that even today have the sound of a rolling oratorio — I could put a stop to that! For chasing me away. "Go away," said Uncle Fedor. So I wouldn't listen. They thought I didn't know. When the last of the noodles were cooked and strained, the soup on the table, Pap would give me a nod. The moment was mine. Stepping up to the hall door, I began:

> The evening meal is served.
> Feathers black and burned.

That did it, as I knew it would. The talk ceased immediately. There followed a shuffling of feet, the putting on of shoes, the scraping of chairs over wood floors, a quick run down the stairs, then a voice saying, as I knew it would:

> Feathers burnt and black?
> I'll get you for that.

That was Uncle Fedor, already running to catch me, as I knew he would, and I, squealing, "Feathers black and burned," running for the safety of the outer door, where, expectantly, I was caught, tossed into the air, caught and tossed up again.

By then, the men were all in the kitchen, each taking his place at the table. Each took his turn with the ladle and the knife, and as they ate, the day's events were told and retold.

Sometimes things went too far, and always it was Uncle Fedor who was the cause of it. Once he brought home a device that, when placed on a chair and unwittingly sat upon, made a most embarrassing sound, and because Gavaj wasn't down yet — Gavaj was always the last to come down — he placed it on Gavaj's chair. If Pap had seen, I know he would not have permitted it, but Pap was busy helping Mama with supper.

When Gavaj walked into the kitchen, all became quiet. But all became quiet no matter when he walked into the kitchen. They respected him. Everybody did. As he made his way to his chair, slowly, as he always did, as he began to sit down, I squeezed my eyes shut. Maybe nothing would happen. But it did. That sound! It wouldn't stop. And the laughter. It wouldn't stop. Some of the men had to wipe their tears away. All but Uncle Fedor. He just sat there eating his soup as if nothing had happened. *How could he?*

For one thing, Gavaj was an older man and no one did that to an older man. And another thing: He was big. Like a bear. He could whip anybody if he wanted to, but even that wasn't it. Maybe it was because he always sat at the head of the table. He was given that respect. Or maybe because he never sat around in his undershirt. Maybe it was because he could read and write. I don't know. But nobody would have done that to him. Why did Uncle Fedor?

Slowly, the laughter petered out, and slowly, Gavaj began to rise from his chair. Looking straight at Uncle Fedor — and for a long time I wondered how he knew it was him — he said, slowly, "You can eat now. You've already thanked the Lord." With these words, he left the table.

Later Pap had a talk with Uncle Fedor. "We must respect our elders. They were here before we were. They are all we have."

Once I asked Uncle Fedor, "Did you ever do anything bad when you were little?" At once I knew I shouldn't have asked him that, but he just laughed.

"I was a boy wasn't I? And boys can be bad. Many were the times I knelt with my brothers." He smiled, remembering, then went on. "But there is one sin that will never go away."

I caught my breath. *What could that have been?*

"I was walking alone one afternoon," Uncle Fedor continued, "nothing to do. And there was this old man sitting by the side of the road. I saw him all right but pretended not to. Deliberately kicking at a few stones, I walked right past him.

"'No,' he cried.

"I stopped, lifted my eyes, looked at his root-like feet, upward to his equally gnarled hands, to the tips of his stringy gray beard, and could look no further. I felt the blood rush to my face. Instinctively, my head, heavy with shame, bowed to him.

"'*Bachi*,' I whispered, then louder so he could hear. Only then was I free to go on.

"I did a lot of bad things, Annie, but that is the only one about which I am still ashamed. Always revere the old ones, Annie. Without them, we wouldn't be here."

Now, Pap was saying the same thing to him: "We must have respect for our elders."

Why did Uncle Fedor do that? I liked Gavaj, too, and I liked Uncle Fedor.

Years later, remembering the fun I had with Uncle Fedor, especially remembering being tossed up into the air, I asked Mama, "Why did he quit tossing me in the air?"

Mama looked at me, a little startled. "You remember that?"

"Oh, yes. I used to beg him, but he walked away. Why did he walk away?"

That's when Mama told me something. "Yes, Uncle Fedor enjoyed tossing you up into the air, and you loved it. One evening you just wouldn't let him stop. When finally he set you down, your eyes were crossed.

"Just a week earlier, your father had an accident at work. He lost an eye. And now this. I began to scream. You began to scream. Pap tried to quiet you, and when he finally did, when he tried talking to you, you couldn't talk. And the next day, and the next — you still couldn't talk. And your left eye never straightened."

"Oh, Mama. I didn't know anything was wrong with me. I remember not being able to talk. But I could sing, Mama. Remember? When setting up the ironing board, the first thing I did was prop up a songbook. By the time I came to the sheets and towels, on the wings of *The Dove*, I had flown all over Spain and back. I had walked through all the rye in Scotland, and when I finally came to the last rough pieces, I was ironing to *Funiculi, Funicula*.

"Yes, I remember. When you sang, everybody listened."

"And I danced. Every time Uncle Fedor played his accordion, I danced."

"And again you wouldn't leave him alone — couldn't wait for him to bring his accordion down. Once he said, 'I'll fix her. I'll play until she drops.' Well, it was he who almost dropped."

"But he was never tired of telling stories. Every night a different one."

Story Time

Wintertime was story time and Uncle Fedor was the one who could tell them — after supper, everyone there: Aunt Julie, Uncle Maksim, and Little Julie, Aunt Liza, Uncle Jakub and Little Liza. We heard *Sniho-Bila* (Snow White), *Tsinderela*, and *Ali Baba* before we heard them in English. There were spine-tingling stories that sent us scurrying to the safety of the chimney corner where, so long as the tea kettle whistled, nothing could hurt us.

There were stories with a moral to them, like the one about Liska. She was the prettiest girl in the village; all the young men wanted her. Instead she went off with a handsome rich man who came riding into the village on a beautiful black horse. First he bought her shoes, then took her to a castle high in the Tatar Mountains and sucked her blood.

"Don't look for riches," was Uncle Mike's admonition.

Beware of the man with fancy ways.
He'll lay to waste your tender face.
A poor man's like a piece of bread.
What's more: he'll keep you warm in bed.

"Marry a poor man," he said to me.

"Oh, I will, I will." (And I did.)

There were stories that resolved daily problems with comic relief, like the one about the man who had a shrew for a wife. There was no end to her displeasure. He began to spend his time listening to the chickens — began to understand their language.

One evening after an ear-splitting harangue, further aggravated by no response on his part, she finally ran out of words. Nothing was heard but the soft clucking of the hens, and the now-and-then crowing of the rooster.

All at once the man burst into laughter.

"Now what are you laughing at?" she cried.

How could he tell her? The rooster had just said, "Why is it? I have all these wives and can control each one. He has but one and can't do a thing!"

Even Gavaj laughed at that story.

Most of the time Gavaj stayed upstairs; if we became noisy he would pound on the floor. "A man can't even pray in this house," he would shout. Once Uncle Fedor shouted back, "If you were down here with us you wouldn't have to pray so much."

"*Czicho,*" said Pap.

One evening Gavaj stayed downstairs. Because he had a story to tell. Gavaj's story:

Two Brides and Two Brothers

Time had come for two brothers to be inducted into the Service; time had come to begin looking for two brides. The period was Lent; time for two weddings right after Easter.

As luck would have it, in the next village were two sisters. A *starosta* was procured, meetings were arranged, dowries decided upon. As orderly as the ringing of a church bell, two marriages were arranged, two weddings took place. Two weeks after nuptials, the brothers were off to honor king and country, the brides left behind to await their return.

Life in the village fell quickly into day-to-day routines: Each bride, for the most part, was left to her own devices. But not for long. The brides, though sisters, were as different as night from day. Ilka was the quiet one, the industrious one, busy with the concerns of hut and her fields. Properly and sedately she waited for the return of her husband. But Zushka! Any gathering, any happening, and she was there.

What really began to bother the village matrons was that when Zushka had a job to be done — a fence to be mended or a tree removed — she easily managed to get one of the village men to do the job for her. "My roof is leaking and there he is, taking care of her roof," was an oft-repeated lament.

Even the postman. When letters came for the two, Ilka took her letter quietly into her hut, but Zushka! "She's more attracted to the carrier," was another remark.

At first annoyed, the women became audibly angry. "Just wait until her soldier comes home. He'll show her a thing or two. He'll show her who's boss."

And they waited, one year, two years. In due time, the brothers returned. In proper manner, they were greeted by the villagers, and in proper manner, each couple retired into their own hut. Patiently the village women waited.

They didn't have long to wait, and what they observed they could never understand. Zushka's husband accompanied her to every gathering, to every happening. When she laughed, he laughed with her. While Ilka's husband, more and more, was seen spending his time at the tavern, with the men. Where was Ilka? Nobody saw her. And no wonder. To whom could she say that one evening after a stay much longer than usual at the tavern, her husband came home, looked into every corner of their hut, then at his wife. "This place is so clean," he said, "there is not a spot into which I can spit. So I'll spit on the shoddiest thing here. I'll spit on you."

But nobody laughed. Not even Aunt Liza.

Gavaj's stories were never funny. Even when people were congratulating a groom — wishing him well — what did Gavaj say? Albeit with a smile on his face: "Beat her. If she's bad, beat her until she is good; if she is good, beat her so she stays good." No. Gavaj could not tell a funny story.

Uncle Mike once said, "Maybe he's like that because his Marcia left him; went back to the Old Country. When he came home from work one day, she was gone."

"Who could live with him?" said Uncle Fedor.

"He sends her money every month," said Uncle Mike, defending him.

No matter, we liked Gavaj.

Sometimes one of the other men would tell a story: Uncle Mike's always began with *"Bulo co nje bulo* (it was what never was)," about a giant who lived in the forest and if you weren't out by nightfall, he'd crush you with one big foot.

Olejar liked to tell scary stories, about little invisible people who lurked in every dark corner of the kitchen, but as long as the tea kettle whistled at the back of the stove, they couldn't hurt you.

Sometimes Pap told a story, but his story was always the same: the one about potatoes.

Pap's Story

There was this young bride. And no matter how hard she tried, she could never please her husband. No matter what, his mother did it better. Even to the potatoes.

She mashed them, she whipped them, she coddled them. *"O, Hospodi,"* she would pray, "please, please."
And always, "Good, but my mother's were better."

Once, disaster struck. A ruckus in the chicken coop. She ran to see what the problem was. A stray rooster had wandered in, frightening the hens out of their nests.

"Out, out," she cried, waving her apron, then, with her apron, began coaxing the hens back into their nests. *"Kuvochki mojo,"* she crooned, commiserating on the lot of the female in general. Then she began to smell something.

"*O, Hospodi!*" she cried. "My potatoes." She ran, but it was too late. The water had all boiled away.

Quickly she tipped the pot to drain out the water but there was no water. Just blackened potatoes. Even the pot was black.

She saved what she could, mashed what she could, and when her husband came home she sat the potatoes on the table, herself went to the loom. *If he'll kill me, he'll kill me*, she thought.

"Aren't you going to eat?" he asked.

"I'm not hungry."

"Well, I am. I could eat the tail of a horse."

"Hail Mary, full of grace," she murmured. "If I die, I die."

All at once a shout "At last! This is the way my mother made potatoes!"

Always the same story, and always, we laughed.

Once Uncle Fedor began a story that lasted until Lent. Every evening he began where he left off then stopped at the most exciting part, and no amount of begging could make him go on.

And now, dear folk, enough I've said.

Time everybody went to bed.

until the last Sunday before Lent.

Everbody came. Even the Donelkos. Even Gavaj came down. He must have really heard all the stories upstairs, and when it came to the end, he just had to come down. He listened with us.

" . . . and when the Prince found the beautiful Ilonka," continued Uncle Fedor, "her captors finally in chains, he swept her up onto his white horse, and, amid the cheers of the happy villagers, rode away to his castle high in the Tatar Mountains." And that was it. THE END.

But nobody wanted the story-telling to end; not even Gavaj.

"One more," he said.

This story is about a woman who always had to have her own way: in what she did, and what she said. She drove her husband out of his mind.

One day, walking along the bank of some running water, her husband commented, "The grass needs mowing."

Without the blink of an eyelash, "The grass needs cutting" she said.

"The grass needs moving," countered her husband.

"The grass needs cutting," was her firm response.

"Mowing," said the husband.

"Cutting," said the wife.

"Mowing,"

"Cutting,"

"Mowing,"

"Cutting,"

"If you say 'cutting' one more time," said the husband, I'll — I'll push into that water.

"Cutting," she said.

Thoroughly enraged, the husband swooped up his wife and threw her into the running stream.

"Cutting," she cried as she sailed through the air.

"Cutting," she cried as she hit the water.

"Cutting," she cried as she began to disappear.

Then, with only her hand out of water, with her fingers, she made cutting movements until they, too, disappeared.

"Thus," said Gavaj, "ends our *Faschengi* (Mardi Gras). Tomorrow Lent begins. Tomorrow we tell bible stories.

And the next evening, as soon as the dishes were done, as soon as Mary, Mikie, and me had finished our praying, as soon as we finsihed our obeisance before each boarder, we scooted under the table and waited for the bible stories to begin. Aunt Julie and Uncle Maksim, Aunt Liza and Uncle Jakub, Little Liza and Little Julie were already there.

(Here, I will interject. The following oft-told stories, originally heard from the pulpit, by the lettered, for the lettered, became altered, even as a garment, originally fashioned for another, is altered to fit the new wearer. The Slavic peasant heard these stories, carried them home in his memory, then retold them in his own words.)

Gavaj's Story

Peter was Jesus' favorite disciple, which is why they spent so much time walking about the countryside. One hot day they came upon a young girl dipping water out of a well.

"Young maiden," asked Peter, "will you be so kind as to give two tired travelers a drink of your water?"

The young girl responded generously.

After Peter and Jesus had traveled a while, Peter began, "That young lady back there, the one who gave us the water, surely you will think of a reward for her?"

"I have thought about it," said Jesus. "Do you recall seeing that lazy fellow lying under a pear tree, too lazy to even pick up one pear?"

"Oh, yes," cried Peter. "So lazy he laid there with his mouth open, waiting for a pear to drop in. What about him?"

"I've been thinking about him, too. What will become of him? Now I have the answer. He will be that young girl's husband."

"Her husband? That kind and generous girl?"

"Peter, Peter. You could never be God. Can't you see? What would happen to the world if lazy married lazy?"

"Now I'll tell one," said Uncle Maksim.

Uncle Maksim's Story

One day Peter said to Jesus, "I'm getting tired of always being Peter. Why can't I be Jesus for a while and You be Peter?"

"Very well," said Jesus. "I'll be glad to be Peter if you'll be Jesus. Now you are God."

Things went along as before — until they came to a small field where a distraught woman was trying to drive her scattered sheep into a pen. A storm was brewing. Many of her sheep appeared to be lost.

"How will you find them?" said Jesus who was Peter to the woman.

"No need to worry," said the woman. "They'll come home. God will find them for me."

Jesus who was Peter, looked at Peter who was Jesus.

"You heard what she said," said Peter who was Jesus.

"I think I would rather go back to being Peter," said Jesus who was Peter.

"And now," said Uncle Jakub, "I will tell one."

Uncle Jakub's Story

One long day, with nothing to eat, Peter began to think that God didn't have to eat. When he began to detect the heavenly aroma of food cooking from one of the huts, he said, "I'm going in."

Jesus didn't mind at all. That was what Peter liked about Jesus. The more Peter let Jesus have his way, the more Jesus let Peter have his way. There was no reason for Peter to have let himself stay hungry for so long.

Inside the hut a young mother was finishing up a small pan of little cakes.

In the voice of a penitent — and Peter was good at that — he began, "Dearest lady, I am very sorry to bother you, but I have been traveling for low these many hours. I haven't had a lick to eat today. Would you be so kind as to let me have just one of those little cakes?"

The lady looked at Peter, at her meager supply of cakes.

These cakes must last me and my children a week she thought; still, maybe I could let him have one. She gave Peter one of the larger cakes.

"Thank you, thank you," cried Peter, adding, "I will share this with my friend, outside, another penitent."

At once the lady cried, "There is another? Here, a cake for him, too."

Once outside, Peter shared all right — he shared the one cake.

The other he hid under his arm. For later, he thought, meaning later for himself. Jesus will never even notice.

After a short period, still hungry, Peter reached for the other cake but there was no cake. Not anywhere. The cake, alas, must have crumbled away.

"What seems to be the matter, Peter?" asked Jesus.

"Oh, nothing. Nothing at all."

"WHAT'S THE MATTER, PETER?"

He knows, Peter thought.

But with God, nothing is wasted. At every place the crumbs had dropped, mushrooms began to appear. And that is why, to this day, we have mushrooms.

Everyone laughed. Even Gavaj. "One more," he said.

Gavaj's Story

At the crucifixion of our Lord, among the bystanders was a gypsy. He winced at every driven nail. But a gypsy will always spot an opportunity. When one of the nails dropped to the ground, he quickly retrieved it and hid it under his tongue. *One less nail*, he thought. One less pain for Jesus.

And that is why, to this day, a gypsy has a golden tongue.

That ended storytelling. We were all beginning to yawn. Merka and Mikie and Little Julie were already asleep under the table. But no.

"One more story," said Uncle Fedor, "then we go."

Uncle Fedor's Story

Jesus must have liked it here on earth because after He died, He continued to come back. But always as an old man.

One day, walking along a country road that wound around a turbulent creek, He thought to test His people: He would ask for help to cross this angry bit of water.

He approached a group of ladies who appeared to be laughing at another lady ahead of them.

"Will one of you please help an old man to cross that stream?"

"Ha," they laughed in unison.

The next to be asked was a young couple. They pretended not to hear Him.

Walking still further He came upon a group of young men busy testing their strength at wrestling. *Surely one of them will help Me*. He should have known better.

"Did you hear Him?" cried one.

"As if we had nothing better to do," said another.

Nearby, a witness to this, was a man, leaning against a tree trunk. It was obvious he had had too much at the tavern.

"*Bachi,*" he said. "I will help you."

That is why, to this day, when a drunk man falls, he will never get hurt.

And everyone agreed.

Mama brought out the last of the pork pieces, sliced up some bread and everybody ate, because the next day began the Great Fast. Meat only on Sunday.

The Lenten Season,
Preparation for Easter

Eating during Lent was a ritual in itself. Soup every day: lentil, or bean, or potato, thickened with *zapraska;* or haluski, rolled out the size of a bread board, then torn, cut, crimped, or spooned into boiling water, drained, then mixed with either sauteed cabbage or sauerkraut, and if you were still hungry, in the pantry, always, a crock of pickled herrings.

Evenings were taken up with the rosary every Monday, Wednesday and Friday — the five Sorrowful Mysteries: how Jesus sweat blood for us, how He was scourged for us, how He was crowned with thorns for us, how He carried the cross for us, how He was crucified for us, then waiting for those who had gone to church, to hear what the priest said.

By Palm Sunday, not only was the house in shining order, so was every soul, and if just one tiny shred of sin still adhered, Holy Week took care of that. Church on Monday, Tuesday, Wednesday, then the dreaded Thursday: twelve men lined up in front of the altar, each holding a candle — the one in the center, the thirteenth, the Great Trojca — and as portions of the Gospel were chanted, one candle was extinguished until only the Trojca was left. When the priest finally came to the part, ". . . filled a sponge with vinegar and gave Him a drink," it, too, was extinguished, leaving the church in total darkness. The beating of a drum, like distant thunder, began. More and more drums, rising to an ear-splitting crescendo, then slowly, slowly, dying away. Two and a half hours, the service took.

Relief could be felt throughout the church, because the next day was Good Friday. No services. Jesus was finally crucified. All we had to do was walk on our knees from the back of the church to the front, reach over and kiss His Face, then, still on our knees, still facing the altar, back again. Lent was, at last, over.

Our Easter dresses were already made, mine and Mary's the same, with violet flowers all over. We also had new shoes, patent leather, and soda pop, all kinds, in the cellar.

Even the mothers were excited, you could tell, because the next day, Easter Saturday, was for baking and cooking. Before the sun was up, Mama already had our dough rising: for the pascha, for the rolls and for the cheesecakes; the ham and kolbassi cooked on top of the stove, then running to Aunt Julie's or Aunt Liza's for eggs, or more flour, and the Donelkos into everybody's house for something because they never had enough of anything. Every house smelled like Easter.

On Easter Sunday, it was every father's duty to carry the basket, and no one was more proud, unless it was Uncle Maksim. Aunt Julie had the most beautiful cover: a cross embroidered entwined with lilies. Once in church it was hard to keep your mind on the glorious resurrection — the smell of all that food — baskets and basketfuls. And when the service was over, each basket was grabbed up, because the last one home would have bad luck all year.

When we could eat no more, Uncle Fedor brought down his accordion and we danced, ran up to Aunt Julie's and Aunt Liza's, back down again, ate some more, sang and danced, then bedtime, because the next day, Easter Monday, was even better than Easter Sunday. All the ladies — little girls, too — were dowsed with water, a delightful and hilarious ritual from our pagan past, a remembrance to Voda (water), the goddess of fertility. Extra supplies of dry clothing were in readiness for that day, and if a man happened to forget, in his exuberance, even one lady, even her husband was insulted.

On Tuesday, the third day of Easter, just to get even, or maybe to continue the fun, the women dowsed the men with pails of water, the men running for their lives.

Once, a bucketful, aimed at Uncle Fedor, missed and hit the kerosene lamp on the kitchen mantel, exploding it. That was it. Easter was over.

About Bread

On a rainy day, Mama loved to bake, and if she knew ahead that it would rain on the next day, before she went to bed, she made a huge batch of dough. When the kneading was finished — it took a half hour — she rolled the dough into a big pan, blessed it, covered it, blessed it again, then set it on the pantry table, where it was cool, to rise.

By morning, the dough was rolling out of the pan; she had to punch it down again, then, as soon as Pap and the men had left for work, as soon as the baby had been nursed and was back to sleep again, as soon as Mary and Mikie were up, and as soon as we had all eaten, she began.

First, because sometimes we were out of bread, Mama made a few small rounds, flattened out, called *poplanki*, to be eaten that day. Mrs. Fontinello made them, too, but she called hers *pizza*. Sometimes Mama and Mrs. Fontinello exchanged.

Once Mama made ours with sauteed cabbage like the Braddock ladies did, and Gavaj scolded her. He said it was a sin to mess with daily bread. Fancy bread was only for Christmas and Easter.

After the *poplanki* had been set aside to rise, Mama began on the bread.

Perfect rounds she made, shaped like cobblestones. She worked fast. As she shaped each round, she blessed it, rolled it into a pan, blessed it again. When all the pans were filled, all in a row on a shelf at the back of the stove, she blessed them all again, then covered them to rise, and when she heard Uncle Mike coming home from work she jumped to the door to keep him from slamming it. So the dough wouldn't drop.

"I knew. I already heard Elijah — heard the thunder."

Mary and I ran to the window to listen, and he was right. Elijah's chariot wheels were bumping all over God's heaven — all over His cobblestones.

"Won't be long now," said Uncle Mike.

We knew what he meant, and again he was right. When Elijah was right over our house, he stopped his chariot and jumped off to relieve himself. That's what made the rain come down.

"And that's what makes the wheat grow," said Uncle Mike, taking a peek at Mama's dough, "so we can have bread — bread with butter, and bread with jelly."

"For when somebody comes, too" I added. I never missed a chance to prove I, also, knew something.

"Yes, for when somebody comes."

And always, somebody came.

The People Who Came

When somebody came, Mama always brought out a loaf of bread. First she blessed it with the knife — because bread is holy — then she cut in. Always, there was somebody coming to our house: the Jewish peddler, the Arabian lady, the umbrella man, and Mr. Bednarik, the order man. And I mustn't forget Uncle George. We never knew when Uncle George was coming. He always came during the night; when morning came I heard him pray; I knew his voice.

We liked when the Jewish peddler came — heard him before we saw him. First we heard the gate, then as he walked past the kitchen window we heard him sing — to the chant of "*Da Veseljatsja Nebesnaja*" (Let the Heavens Rejoice):

> Something for your rhue,
> Your hind-end, too.

(The humor here maybe lost to the non-Rusyn reader. The chant, the Jewish merchant was using is from the Byzantine mass.)

By the time he walked into the kitchen, we were already laughing. Those words. To a church chant.

He had dark hair that curled down over one side of his forehead and his hat was always jammed against the back of his head. His necktie was thrown back over his shoulder, his coat was always flying open, and when he snapped open his bag, he swooped his head down inside, then, BOO, right in my face, as I knew he would, then slowly began taking out the bottles, one at a time, holding each one up so we could see the colors, again singing. "Something for your rhue." Mama always bought one of those. Then she bought *sosborses*, something only for ladies, and liniment for the men.

The very last things out of the bag were little glass lanterns, glass dolls, little dogs, all filled with real candy. Mama bought one for each of us. Then, holding onto our treasures, we watched the peddler carefully put everything back into his bag.

But once he reached for our Merka — made like he would put her into his bag, too. I screamed, "No!" After that, when he came, I hid Merka in the pantry and stayed with her until he left. I didn't like him anymore.

Then there was Mr. Bednarik, the order man, always with a pencil behind one ear, and no matter how many times I tried, I could never hold a pencil behind my ear. Every morning he came, sitting down at the same place at the table. Mama already had a spot cleared.

First, he gave the news: if somebody was going back to the Old Country, if somebody just came. If somebody had a baby, or if a baby died, or if somebody's boy fell off a swing and broke his leg. Then he took Mama's order. Pork steak for breakfast and for lunches, beef plate with a "big bone for soup," always potatoes, and beans, and cabbage, and always at the end, gingersnaps. Then he had to go.

"Have to hurry," he always said, so the orders could be made up and delivered in time for all the suppers.

But when the *Rabjanka* (the Arabian lady) came, she stayed awhile, so glad to slide the pack off her back.

"*Oj, joj,*" she'd say, straightening up, stretching her back, then flopping into a chair. "Every day, heavier."

She was a jolly lady, with golden earrings, a flowered scarf on her head, and when she pulled off her scarf there were wet ringlets all across her forehead.

Again, Mama cleared off a spot on the table, but for her — a cup of tea and bread with jelly. "Have some tea," said Mama.

"Oh yes, oh yes," cried the Arabian lady. Not until she had finished her tea and her bread did she begin to open her pack.

So many things she had: curtains and tablecloths, ribbons and lace, dress goods to make things. The striped was for dresses and the flowered for aprons. Black, if somebody died.

She measured the cloth from the tip of her fingers to the tip of her nose, the tip of her fingers to the tip of her nose and I always wondered: Because she had a big nose, did it make any difference in the measurement?

Mama also bought for the men: work shirts or Sunday shirts, underwear or socks. Socks were only for Sundays: For everyday use, the men wrapped their feet in squares of cloth brought from the Old Country called *onuchki*.

And she didn't tease us. She gave us each a piece of candy and always for Mama, a handkerchief. When she began folding her things back into her bag, Mama helped her, and when she slipped the pack over her shoulder, "*Oj, oj,*" she moaned, "always heavier." When I grew up, I thought, I must remember not to become an Arabian lady.

Then the beggars. Every payday. There was an old lady, hunched over, and an old man with a cane. When they got something, each raised an arm to heaven and prayed for us, and if the beggar got extra he would kneel down in the middle of the kitchen and pray. Every payday they came.

The organ grinder came on payday, too, with a monkey on his shoulder. Even the mothers ran out to see him. Because he told fortunes. As the organ grinder played, his monkey passed out fortune cards, but first you had to put a dime into his paw. Then he handed you a card, and when the card was read, everybody laughed.

"You will find some money."

"You will meet a dark man. Beware. Do not believe him."

"You will take a long trip."

"Yes, into the cellar to wash clothes," the women said.

But they believed him.

Then the rag man. All the kids waited for him. Regularly, the sounds of evening were broken by his chant: *"Schrreps en rrex"* (scraps and rags), and we'd scatter, each to a hidden cache, then stand in line, clutching our precious bundles to be weighed. For just rags you got a penny, for scraps of metal maybe a nickel, but for a piece of copper — the men sometimes found pieces of copper on the railroad — a dime.

The money was hoarded for when the ice cream wagon came. We heard the CLANG, CLANG before we saw the wagon. By the time it came to our corner, we were there: a jumping, squealing group. What shall it be? Already I could taste the strawberry. Vanilla had a taste you wished would go on forever, and chocolate — just the sound of the word and you could feel it sliding down your throat. Your decision, finally made, was never, ever, quite the right one, but once made, once it was presented in that most heavenly of creations, a thin, crisp, waffle-like concoction twirled into the shape of a cone, everything in the world was right. And no matter how long you tried to make it last, it didn't. Only the memory lasted.

One thing more: the circus. When the circus came, it was Uncle Fedor who took us. We each got two nickels: one for popcorn and one for root beer. I used mine for the merry-go-round, spacing my two rides so they'd last longer, then for the rest of the evening, I stood, eyes riveted on the prancing horses until it seemed it was I going around and around, and when we got home, when I finally got to bed, it seemed I was on the merry-go-round, going round, and around, and around. . . .

Then when we got bigger, Kennywood Park.

But of all the people who came — and he wasn't even a people, he was our Uncle George — we liked Uncle George the best. He always brought us something.

Uncle George

If it hadn't been for Uncle George, Pap wouldn't be here. Uncle George was the first in their family to come to America; first him, then Aunt Julie. When he had enough money saved, he went back, paid Pap's fare to come here, himself staying to get married.

Uncle George and Aunt Ersa lived with Grandma for as long as it took for him to put up a new hut. In proper order, he fathered a girl, a boy, and a girl, enjoying, even flaunting, his status as an *Americanec*. But he missed America and decided to return. Ersa, unfortunately for her, decided on staying behind. Uncle George came back alone, to board at our house.

But he didn't stay long — looked for another place to stay — a bigger town than Wall.

He not only didn't stay very long at one house, he didn't stay very long at one job. Once a little money found its way into his pockets, he was out to reconquer America. He began with Braddock, where, alas, the arenas for his conquests never got further than the nearest tavern. That was why Uncle George appeared regularly at our house, without a cent, without a job.

Pap would scold him, "When are you going to send Ersa some money?"

"Next time," he would say.

He always brought us things. The very first gramophone we had, Uncle George got it for us. It came with two recordings: "The Black Forest Polka," to which we danced, and the other was something from *Aida,* and when the spring broke, I twirled the discs with my finger. *Aida* became my one and only introduction to opera.

We never knew when Uncle George would come — always during the night — probably in no condition for us to see — but when morning came I knew he was there. I could pick out his voice. In the hubbub of early morning sounds, the grumbling, the praying, the shuffling of shoes, then the sounds of cheery "good mornings" downstairs in the kitchen, he, left alone upstairs, still in prayer, I heard him.

> And now, dear Mother, ever kind,
> Guard the ones I left behind —
> My wife and children. Ask your Son,
> That someday we will live as one.

Look kindly on my brother, here.
His wife and all his children dear.
On friends, and every neighbor-host.
Give to each whatever's most.

As for me, another day.
Is all I ask, and, if I may —
Oh, dearest Mother, please don't fret —
A little glass of bourbonette.

Unfortunately, the little glass of bourbonette often landed Uncle George in jail, with Pap having to go to Braddock to bail him out.

Then we didn't see him anymore.

"*Do Jungston* (To Youngstown)," someone said.

"Now I'll never find him," said Pap.

Our Yard

E veryone had a fenced-in yard, a boardwalk that went around from front to back with a gate at each end. A water pump not far from the kitchen door, and somewhere at the back of the yard, hidden from view by tall sunflowers, an outside toilet. When you saw the sunflowers, you knew where to go.

At the rain spout side of the house was a rain barrel for washing hair, then over from the kitchen door was a mud scraper.

Everybody had a garden. Because we lived in a corner house, we also had the use of a piece of ground that belonged to the Pennsylvania Railroad Company. That's where our garden was. Which is why in the yard proper, we had an enclosure for chickens and one for pigs.

The garden was Pap's pride and joy. Every evening after supper, that's where he spent his time. Sometimes he let me go with him. I knew where not to step.

There was parsley for soup, dill for cottage cheese, beets for special occasions, lots of lettuce, and radishes and kohi-rabi. When the kohi-rabi was right, the men ate it right out of the garden.

And garlic to rub on toast or on your chest if you had a cold.

And onions. As soon as the green tops were high enough, on wash days, Mama would break off a few, give us each a cup of soapy water, and we'd blow through the hollow onion tops, making bubbles in the air.

Along the front boardwalk we had hollyhocks and four-o-clocks. We weren't allowed to play there, but we could on the other side where the rain spout was. Especially after a rain, that was the best spot. We made mud pies, little cakes with beer caps pressed into them and gingerbread men. Stones for money.

Once we made the mud too soft, so we just squished it around until Mikey got some in his eye and began to cry. After I cleaned him up — Mary pumped the water and I cleaned — we had to go into the house and kneel for penance.

We played hopscotch on the sidewalk, or tag, using the pump for home base, or hide-and-go-seek. So many places to hide!

Over from the toilet, on the opposite side of the back gate, was a small wood and coal shed, an enclosure made of railroad ties for pigs, and up from that, one for chickens. When it was time for them to eat, the harrumphing from the pigs and the raucous noise from the chickens sounded "like an army beating its drum," said Uncle Fedor. When finally fed, the last slurp-slurp from the pen, combined with the clucking of the hens, was an evening's song.

This was the best of times for me: Pap and I just sitting there, not saying a word, just listening to the pigs, to the chickens, to the sound of men talking — sounds forever tucked into my memory. Sounds meant to be broken.

"Time to go," said Pap. "I'll race you to the house." And always, as I knew I would, I beat him, until one day...

Supper was over, the pigs and chickens fed, Pap and the men just talking on the porch, when two men approached our house. I had never seen them before.

They opened the gate, stopped to look at the pigs, then began walking toward us. Pap rose to meet them.

"I see you have pigs," said one of them.

"Yes," replied Pap. "I hev pigs. You vant see? Com."

Pap and the men walked toward the pigpen.

"Why do they want to see our pigs?" I asked.

"Maybe they want to buy," said Uncle Mike.

"No," I cried. I flew through the yard and stopped hard against the pigpen gate.

One of the men was prodding the pigs with a long stick, making them squeal.

"Don't do that!" I cried. He didn't even look at me, just kept right on poking with his stick, so I grabbed the stick and began to kick him, hard.

"No, no, Annie," said Pap, but I wouldn't stop. He had to pick me up and carry me back into the house. "Keep her here," he said to Mama.

But I wouldn't stay. Mama couldn't hold me.

"Annie, we have to sell the pigs," said Pap. "They are getting too big. No room for them. And Mama needs the money. Those new shoes — with all those buttons? Mama has to pay for them."

"Take the shoes back."

Next morning my mind was a clean slate again. I had forgotten about the pigs. Not until it was time to feed them did I see that the pigs were gone. All but the little one.

"No pigs? Only Snooky?"

"Yes. Only Snooky. Aren't you glad? No pigs to push her around any more. Now she can eat all she wants."

Pap was right. Every day, all Snooky did was eat and sleep, then eat some more until she could hardly move.

One morning, Mama said, "Stay in bed. Watch Mary and Mikey."

After she left, she closed the door. I opened it. There was no one in the kitchen, but I could hear shouts from the outside. I opened the door to see. Everybody was down in the pigpen: Uncle Mike, Uncle Fedor, Pap and Mama. Uncle Mike was holding a knife, and Snooky, squealing, was backing away from him. I ran down to stop him.

"Stop it!" I shouted. But nobody heard me.

Then something happened. Uncle Mike slipped in the mud. Snooky leaped over him right into Uncle Fedor, knocking him over, straight through the gate where Pap was standing and knocked him over, too. There they all were, in the mud, Snooky out of the pen not knowing which way to go.

"Run, Snooky, run," I cried, but the men were up and after her. Pap, too. Around and around they chased, yelling and shouting, and Snooky squealing until I couldn't stand it. I began squealing, too. I ran squealing into the house, into the bedroom, into the closet. When Pap came we were all squealing: Mary and Mickie holding onto me and squealing.

After we stopped, he took us all to Aunt Julie's. Aunt Julie gave us bread with jelly and tea, and when Mikie fell asleep, we all played clap hands.

When Pap came to get us, the men had already finished eating.

After we ate, Pap and I walked down to the pigpen. So quiet. All I could hear was the clucking of the chickens.

"Did Snooky run away?"

"No. We still have her. In another way. But first I must tell you a story.

"Back in the Old Country when I was about your age, we also had a little pig. We were poor. We had no father. Grandma had to go out to work, but when I became sick, too weak to walk, became too much for Aunt Julie to handle, Grandma had to stay home. Aunt Julie was just nine. That's when somebody gave us a little pig. Kukla, we called her.

"And I loved Kukla. The way you loved Snooky. Sometimes she was the only playmate I had. And if it weren't for a Jewish family, who every morning sent over potato peelings and other scraps of food, I don't know how Kukla would have survived.

"But she did, every day growing bigger and fatter until she could barely walk. The time had come for the next part of her life."

"Next part?"

"Yes. Everything in life goes through parts. *Natura nasa*. Like the apple. When it's finished growing, it falls from the tree. That part of its life is over. We pick it up and eat it. If we didn't, the apple would rot or dry up and be of no use to anyone.

"So it was with Kukla. One part of her was finished. She was ready for the next. With God nothing is wasted. Grandma sold some parts — got some money — the rest went into sausages, chitlins to mix with potatoes, bacon. We had something to eat through the winter months. By springtime, I was strong again. It was Kukla who fed us. It was Kukla who made me well again.

"So it is with Snooky. She is now in another *sushchestvo*." Pap often used Prayer Book words. "And Mama will take great care of every part of her. We fed Snooky through the summer months, she, in turn, will feed us through the winter months."

"But the knife? I saw Uncle Mike... ."

"Sometimes there has to be a knife. Did you ever watch Mama chop up an onion? She has to use a knife.

"Wheat grows in the field. It is planted, attended to, until finally, full blown and golden in the breeze, it has to be cut down. Otherwise, there'd be no flour. We would have no bread. Another *sushchestvo*.

"Nothing dies; nothing is ever lost. Deep inside your brain sits a little angel on a little shrine called Memory. Everything you do and everything you see is recorded. You have one, I have one, Mama has one. The apple has one. It remembers how to grow fruit again. Next year we'll have more apples. Come spring, we'll have another Snooky. Now let's go: I'll race you to the house."

"Okay." But I didn't feel like running. *Sushshestvo*. The word was God's word, but the knife hurt.

Registration for School

One afternoon — I had just finished rocking the baby to sleep, Mama was busy cupping flour into a bowl for the noodles and talking to Uncle Mike, Mary and I just listening, when a knock came to the door. I ran to see.

It was an English lady. (English is a generic term for people not of foreign extraction.) An English lady, I could tell. She had on white gloves, a hat with daisies all around, and a purse with a gold chain. She was smiling and saying something.

I smiled, too, but I didn't know what to say. When somebody came to our house we said, "*Vitajce u nas* (welcome to our house)," but she was English and English people didn't talk that way. Good thing Uncle Mike was there. He knew English.

"Kom, kom," he said. "Kom in."

The lady, still smiling, said something that sounded like "Tenk-oo." Uncle Mike said "Tenkoo" too, then added, "Pliss kom," and when the lady came into the house, he pulled out a chair and said, "Pliss sit dunn," and again she said "Tenkoo." My first lesson in English: I didn't know what it meant but already I was sounding it out.

And she didn't sit down the way we do: PLUMP. Aunt Julie once plumped down so hard on a chair, she flew one way and broke the chair.

The lady sat down very nicely, then nicely laid her purse on the table. And when she nicely pulled off her gloves, one at a time, there was a ring on her finger, and right then and there I decided: When I grew up, I'd wear a hat with daisies all around and wear a ring on my finger, but where would I get a ring or a hat with daisies? Now the lady was saying something. She had taken a tablet and pencil out of her purse.

"Are you Annie?" she asked, looking directly at me.

Annie? That was me. That's what Mrs. Murray called me. Everybody called me Hancha, sometimes Hanichka, but the Murrays called me Annie.

"Yes. She Annie," said Uncle Mike.

"She is already six?"

"No. She no six yet. She be six in *Marec*."

"Oh, not until March? Then she is too young for school."

"No, no. She no too young. She schmart. Too schmart."

The lady, smiling, turned to me. "Would you like to go to school?"

Uncle Mike looked at me. "*Do scholi?*"

Do scholi? Every morning I watched Julia Murray and her friends hurrying past our house on their way to school, and after they had gone, I too, walked, schoolgirl-fashion, up and down the kitchen floor, pretending. I nodded, trying not to jump.

"Yes," said Uncle Mike. "She go. She schmart. Too schmart."

Mama was also nodding her head.

"Very well," said the lady. "How do you spell her name?"

"Spell?" Uncle Mike didn't know that word.

"How do you write it?" She pretended to write.

"Oh — oh." Uncle Mike understood.

But nobody knew how to write. Or spell. Not Uncle Mike, not Mama. My bright new world was beginning to fall apart.

All at once, Mama thought of something. She ran into the back bedroom, came back with my baptismal certificate, gave it to Uncle Mike. He gave it to the lady. The lady began to write, and when she had finished, she looked at me.

"Annie, you are now a schoolgirl."

What followed — Pap's excitement when he came home, the boarders teasing disbelief – pales before what Mrs. Murray said. When Mama told her she'd have to make me some dresses, she said, "Oh no. You'll have to buy her some dresses."

"B—Buy a dress?"

"Yes. From Mandelblatt's."

Mama bought two: one, blue with white eyelets all over, and another, plaid with a pleated whirly skirt, and every hour, every day, I took a peek at them.

Finally, the first day of school. As soon as the men had left for work, Mama's attention centered on me — began dressing me — new underthings, a new petticoat, the blue dress, new socks and shoes, and "Don't touch me," I kept saying, first to Mary, then to Mikie.

By the time Julia Murray knocked on the door, I was ready, a wicker lunch basket with a handle and a lid on my arm.

Waiting outside were Bridget and Elsie Dugan. All the way, they talked and laughed. I didn't know what they were saying, but when they laughed, I laughed, too. Until we came to the schoolhouse.

Never in my life, before or after, have I seen so big, so grand an edifice. And steps so wide. Then inside: everything so vast, so high, with more steps, high and wide, boys and girls running up, and up, and up.

Many years later, remembering the moment, I was able to pen the following lines:

> The stairs were wide and high,
> Turning higher and higher to where you couldn't
> even see.
> Away up at the turn was a big window. Big.
> And full of sunshine.
> So much sun it splashed across the walls,
> Across the pictures on the walls,
> It tumbled down the stairs.
> So much sun. And so many kids going up and up.

Then someone said to me, "This way. You have to go this way. The first grade is down here, at the foot of the stairs."

Once inside the room, I was taken to a seat at the back, where I sat and watched; so many girls and boys, all running around, all talking at the same time. When a bell rang, all flew into their seats. The teacher closed the door, stood in front of the class, said something, and smiled. I smiled, too.

Then she opened a big book and began to read — the first of many readings I came to know by heart, "green pastures and still waters."

After the reading, everyone's head bent down to the desktop. Mine, too. All recited what later became one of the first things I brought home: "Arr Farre Arrti Yeven" (Our Father Who Art in Heaven).

"*Po Anglicki,*" Mama said to Aunt Julie, proudly.

After prayers, there was writing on the board, but not by me, much talking back and forth, but not by me, much raising of hands, until I began to think: *Maybe I should raise my hand, too.* I did, but when the teacher pointed to me, I froze.

When the bell rang and everybody rose, I fell into line, too. I picked up my lunch basket, marched out, and kept on walking until I got home.

"Why are you home so early?" Mama asked.

"I don't know." I didn't know I had walked out at recess time.

On the next day, when the bell rang, the teacher came out with me. She called to another girl who came and stood beside the teacher. The teacher said something to her — about me, I could tell — then, smiling at both of us, she left. The other kids were running and yelling all around us, but we just stood there looking at each other.

She began to rock back and forth, then reached out and touched my arm.

I touched her arm.

She touched me back.

I touched her back.

We had discovered what a long-ago ancestor learned: the first move toward civilized behavior was to reach out and touch another being.

She tagged me again, hard, and ran. I ran after her, tagged her, but another girl tagged her, too, and she ran after her and I was left standing alone. Something else I learned. Sometimes one stands alone.

Back in the school room, everyone took his own seat. I took mine. And I liked it. I could see and hear everything. And I could sing.

> Oo-vrrah, oo-vrrah, vi sink a zhu-ba-li
> (Hurrah, hurrah, we sing with jubilee.)
>
> Oo-vrrah, oo-vrrah, da len de med a frri
> (Hurrah, hurrah, the land that made us free)

After school, I ran all the way home. Because I missed them. When the kids saw me, they jumped.

"Our Annie's here, our Annie's here."

And all evening I sang, "Oo-vrrah, oo-vrah. . . ."

"*Po Anglicki,*" I heard Mama say to Pap. He smiled.

A Song for Crying

When you're little, you're bad. And you don't even know you've been bad until it's too late, until you get hollered at. But I wasn't feeling good. That's why I didn't want to watch Ilonka, even though Mama was sick. That's why I told the doctor when he came, "Don't bring us any more babies," and that's why Aunt Julie hollered, "You bad, bad girl."

But I was sick, too. The next morning my face was all red and splotchy.

"Measles," said Mrs. Murray.

We all had them, all but Ilonka.

"Keep Ilonka away from them," Mrs. Murray told Mama. And she did.

But when she cried, nobody could make her stop. Nobody knew the right songs. Only I did, but I was sick. I couldn't move. Not my arms, not my legs. And so hot.

But the rain was cool. It fell all over my face and into my mouth and down my throat. Only it wasn't rain. It was Mama putting cool cloths on my face and squeezing water into my mouth.

And when Pap came home from work, he came straight into the bedroom, straight to me. Nobody ever came straight to me.

When finally the blinds were raised, we were allowed to sit up and drink tea, and the tea was good.

That's when Ilonka got away. She ran into our room squealing and jumping, so glad to see us, and we, so glad to see her, but Mama ran in and grabbed her away.

That night, after everybody had eaten, we all had to go upstairs into the back bedroom because, now, our Ilonka had the measles. I saw her face, all red, her eyes closed shut.

When the doctor came, we had to be very quiet. All except Uncle Mike. He was praying, on and on, until we fell asleep.

In the morning, when we awakened, Pap was already in the room with a towel and pan of water to wash us.

"Is it Sunday?" I asked. Sunday was his day to awaken us and wash us, but he didn't answer. He didn't sing "Wake up, wake up, you sleepy head," or anything else. He just washed, first Mikie, then Mary, but not me, because I was still sick. Then he said, "Downstairs. We're going to see Ilonka."

We followed Pap. Pap holding Mikie's hand, into the kitchen, then into Mama's bedroom, and that's when we saw her: Ilonka, her eyes closed, sleeping in Mama's bed, Uncle Mike kneeling beside her. When he saw us he rose and backed away. In the kitchen, Mama began to wail. We didn't know what to do.

Then Pap lifted us, one at a time, first Mikey, to kiss her.

"She's in heaven, now. An angel now," said Uncle Fedor, wiping his eyes.

"Too good for this world, she was," said Uncle Mike. "Too good for us."

Too good for us. I looked at her, so beautiful, so white, and remembered the many times I didn't want to watch her. Didn't even want to sing to her.

But it's hard to sing when you're crying, when you'd rather be outside playing with the kids. Sometimes she cried so hard that no matter how loud I sang, "Marching Through Georgia," she kept right on crying, and now. . .

After breakfast, we all had to go upstairs again, but we could hear everything. We heard when Aunt Julie came in. As soon as she got in the door she began to wail. Then Aunt Liza: As soon as she got in, she began to wail. Soon everybody was wailing, we were too, but we didn't know it — not until Uncle Fedor came up to stop us.

The next time we were allowed downstairs, our Ilonka was gone, the bedroom furniture back to where it had been. Pap was talking to Uncle Mike and Uncle Fedor, and Mama was pouring tea for everyone.

"Pap?"

"Yes, Annie."

"Why did God take her?"

"Maybe He missed her. You know, Ilonka was His little girl before He gave her to us. Maybe He was lonesome."

I tried to imagine God sitting at His table, being lonesome. "Is she up there now? In His kitchen?"

"Yes. Now drink your tea."

But I didn't want my tea. I was imagining Ilonka running and laughing up there in God's kitchen. Was she hiding her face in His lap? Was she making Him laugh? I never saw God laugh.

"Can God laugh?" I asked.

"What a question," said Mama. "Drink your tea already."

But Pap was listening. So was Uncle Mike, and Uncle Fedor.

"Does He know how to make our Ilonka laugh? And can He sing? Does He know the right songs? Does He know "Pop Goes the Weasel"?

"Of course He does. God knows everything." That was Uncle Mike.

"If Ilonka cries, will He know what to do? Will He know that you have to start with the very loudest song – louder than crying — like "Yankee Doodle"? He probably never even heard "Yankee Doodle". Probably didn't even know English. What will He *do* when Ilonka begins to cry?"

"Then, Annie, you'll just have to sing down here," said Pap, "and He'll hear you. Ilonka will hear you, too. But if you cry, she'll hear you and cry with you. Now drink your tea."

"Oh, I'll sing. All the time I'll sing."

But it's hard to sing when you're crying. You have to keep going back to "Marching Through Georgia".

The days went on. Soon it was wintertime, time for stories. Little by little, we began to laugh. Then came Lent. Then Easter.

One evening we were all herded upstairs because the doctor was coming. Mama wasn't feeling very well.

And the following morning when Pap came up with a towel and pan of water for washing, he came in singing:

> Wake up, wake up, you sleepy heads,
> Get out, get out, get out of bed.
> Mama has a cookie made,
> Filled with oats and marmalade.

And when we asked, "Is it Sunday?" he said, "Better than Sunday."

Quickly, we washed up, dressed, then marched downstairs. Already we heard Uncle Mike and Aunt Julie. And I wondered why Aunt Julie was there so early.

"Where's Mama?"

"In here," said Pap, turning us toward the bedroom. There we saw: *Mama holding a little baby.*

"Ours?"

"Ours."

On tippy-toes we were allowed to reach over to see better, to touch her.

"Can she cry?" I asked.

"Wait until you hear. Better get your songs ready."

"Oh, I will, I will."

But all the baby did was sleep.

"When is she going to cry?"

"She will," said Aunt Julie. "And you will, too."

About Ena

Something was going on. I could tell. When old people know something and they're not telling, you could tell, and it wasn't like Easter or Christmas when everybody is talking and laughing at the same time. This was something different.

"Keep the kids quiet," Mama said to me.

Even the boarders, even Uncle Mike: As soon as they had finished with supper, they all went straight upstairs to their rooms.

I could tell by the way Pap was helping Mama, like he *wanted* to help, she sweeping up the floor and he wiping and shining the stove, then standing, waiting for what else to do. Mama was spreading out her best tablecloth, the one she brought from the Old Country. The one embroidered all over with flowers.

"The wine," she was saying to Pap. "And the bacon."

"Mama…?"

"Quiet."

That's when Ena came in, all out of breath.

Ena was Mama's niece.

She was the eldest of a big family, which is why, as soon as she was old enough, Pap sent passage money for her to come to America. She at once got a job working for Mrs. Hessler. The Hesslers owned a grocery store in Wall. Every evening Ena brought us something: the funnies, "Barney Google" and "The Katzenjammer Kids", paper dolls to cut out, and sometimes gingersnaps, but this time there was nothing. Just "Slava Isusu Christu," then she asked, "What shall I wear?"

"The white dress. I have it ready."

The white dress. Ena knew something, too. Everybody but me, so I did what I always did, pretended I knew. "Can I wear my pink dress?"

"What?" said Mama, then turned away as if I weren't even there. As if I didn't know *anything*.

That's when I heard a knock on the door.

"Quickly. Upstairs. Take the kids upstairs."

"But Mama… ."

"*Marsch*," said Pap.

"Okay." When Pap said *marsch*, you marched. "You, too," I said to Mary, pushing her ahead so I could sneak a look back into the kitchen. Two men were standing in the doorway, Pap welcoming, with "*Vitajce u nas.*"

Upstairs, the men were already in their own little world, smoking their pipes and talking, but when they saw us, they stopped.

"M—Mama said to come up," I said defensively. Most of the time when I came up I was told to go back downstairs.

"Did they come?" asked Uncle Mike. He knew something, too.

"Yeah. Somebody. But we had to leave."

"Oh, ho! And you don't like it," said Uncle Fedor. "Just you wait. Someday they'll come for you."

"Me?"

"Yes, you. To get married. Just you wait."

"Married?"

"Yes, you little rabbit. That's why they came. To take Ena away. To get married. As you will, too." He tried to tickle me. "As soon as you're big enough. As soon as you learn to make noodles."

Noodles? Ena was good at making noodles. Better than Aunt Julie, Pap once said. She often helped Mama. And that's why. . .? Those men downstairs. Did they come to take our Ena away?

"As soon as you learn to make noodles," repeated Uncle Fedor.

"Leave her alone," scolded Uncle Mike.

Later, when Mama called for us to come down, I noticed she had tears in her eyes. Ena was in the back room changing clothes. Quickly I asked, "Is Ena going to leave us?"

Just as quickly, Mama reached out to hug me. "Yes, Ena will be leaving us. Ena will be getting married."

"Yes, I know. Because she can make noodles."

"Who told you that? Uncle Fedor."

"Yes. And someday they'll come and get me."

"He was only teasing."

Still, there were tears in her eyes. Throwing my arms around her, I whispered in her ear, "Don't cry, Mama. Nobody is ever going to take me away, because I'm never going to learn how to make noodles."

Despite the tears, our house became the hub of much excitement. The wedding date was set for right after Easter. Dresses had to made. From the Arabian lady, Mama bought flowered lavender voile. Mary and I would be dressed alike, with some extra for a blouse for Mama. The next time the lady came, she brought white satin for Ena, yards of lace, and a cloud of material for a veil — so beautiful I was beginning to have second thoughts about the noodles.

The sewing was done, the walls were painted, woodwork varnished, all curtains washed, stretched and hung, and all the time, "Watch the kids. Watch the kids."

Then the food: kolbassi with sauerkraut, stuffed cabbage with sauerkraut, piles of breaded pork chops. Aunt Julie and Aunt Liza did the baking: little cakes filled with prunes, apricots and cottage cheese. Pap and Uncle Mike took care of the drinks: beer for the men, wine for the ladies, and soda pop, all flavors, for the kids. I thought The Day would never come. Finally . . .

We were already dressed when we heard: *violins*. The gypsies were here! They came from Braddock, from Hawkins Avenue. Every time there was a wedding, they came with their violins, with a sound straight from Heaven. I flew down the stairs.

"Watch the kids."

I know, I know.

But nobody had to watch anybody. Everybody was rushing down the steps to where the gypsies were: outside the kitchen door, playing till you thought your heart would break.

Somehow the kitchen had been cleared, somehow the table had been spread with a pure white cloth. At the center was a loaf of bread and a small bowl of salt.

People began to come in. Then up from the cellar, where they had been cooking, came Aunt Julie and Aunt Liza. Little Julka and Little Lizka were standing with me, the kids holding on. More people came — the Donelkos, Susie squeezing next to me. And all the while, the gypsies, in one corner of the kitchen, plinking at their fiddles, tingling the air like a soda pop when you first opened the bottle.

All at once a hush came over the room. Michael, the bridegroom, followed by his ushers and the *Pitach* (spokesman) entered the kitchen. The violins swung into a triumphant march, a cue for Ena and her bridesmaids to begin coming down from the upstairs, and when she appeared at the doorway, veil over her face, the music exploded with a crash. The groom walked over to Ena. Together they knelt at the table. The *Pitach* moved up to stand behind them. He began:

> There comes a time, the Good Book says,
> A little bird must leave its nest.
> Must say good-bye to carefree ways.
> Must say good-bye to childhood days. *Huzza.*

At the word "huzza," and after each subsequent "huzza," the gypsies, fiddles poised, bows raised, played the saddest refrain heard anywhere. No instrument can cry like a violin.

The *Pitach*, who was now standing directly behind Ena, continued.

First I turn to you, my friends.
I take this time to make amends.
For any hurt or wordless slight.
I know I wasn't always right. *Huzza.*

To aunts and uncles, dear to me.
The many times you shielded me.
I didn't know — was not aware.
You did it just by being there. *Huzza.*

And brothers, far across the sea.
Always, always dear to me.
Times there were I didn't show it.
Brothers, dear I hope you knew it.
You will always be a treasure.
More than I can ever measure. *Huzza.*

Sisters, blessed sisters, dear.
The times we argued without fear,
As if our days would go forever.
Sweet they were: our times together.
And now that time has come to leave you,
Please forgive me if I grieved you. *Huzza.*

Now I turn to Mother, Dad,
Far away in another land,
A world away and yet so near me,
Kneeling here, I know you hear me.
Hear me say: In course of days,
I misbehaved in many ways,
Brought many a tear into your heart,
Unmindful that some day we'd part.
Now it's time to say good-bye.
Forgive me. Please, oh, please, don't cry. *Huzza.*

The effectiveness of the *Pitach* was determined by the copiousness of tears evoked: The more tears, the better his performance.

Happily teared out, all present regrouped — the wedding party into waiting coaches to church, Mama and the ladies to the cellar to the cooking. The kids and I gravitated to the gypsy corner where one fiddler was already playing, Little Julka already dancing. I joined in, squealing and hopping, until Aunt Julie came up to get us.

"Downstairs. Eat."

Downstairs we were each given a roll with butter and a bottle of pop and shooed away. "Outside," because the gypsies had to eat. The table was set for them. We went.

Outside, we at once headed for the street, Little Julka on one side of me, Little Lizka on the other, our Mary and Mikie squealing in and out and around us, glad, I guessed, that I wasn't chasing them away.

"Don't run," I cautioned. "You'll fall and dirty up your nice clothes, and I'll have to clean you up."

"We won't."

That's when Bridget Murray saw us. At once, she ran down to join us. Little Julka and Little Lizka made room for her. We linked arms.

"So much food we have," I said to her. "All kinds. And pop. All kinds. Do you want to come? You can if you want to. Ask your mother?"

That's when we heard the gypsies.

"They're back, they're back. The wedding party is back."

We ran. By the time we reached the house, the best man was already singing:

> Beautiful as a rose she is.
> Power and glory now are his.
> Those whom God hath joined with wonder,
> Let no mortal pull asunder.

But the way into the house was blocked; Aunt Julie and Aunt Liza held a broom across the doorway. *Because of the evil eye.* It must not see the beauty of the bride, the handsome features of the groom, their happiness. It must be diverted, lest it cast a spell on them.

Aunt Julie and Aunt Liza, the door blocked, began to sing:

> Away, away, you ugly things.
> We do not know you. Pray, what brings
> You to this door? Please go away.
> Away. Don't desecrate this Day.

The best man replying:

> What you say is very true.
> Outcasts, we, and ugly, too.
> But once inside, no one will stare.
> None will even know we're there.

To which Aunt Liza replied:

> Well, if you will hide your faces,
> You may come in and take your places:
> Tables set with linens old,
> Stitched with tattered marigold.

With dubious faces — the evil eye must continue to be diverted — Aunt Julie and Aunt Liza removed the barrier of brooms, then, as each member jumped through the door, each got a conk on the head with a broom handle, as did we, following in line: Conk! Conk!

Tables had already been set in both rooms. Aunt Liza and Aunt Julie and Mama were already bringing up the food, Pap and Uncle Mike ready with the wine bottles, but first we had to pray, then a toast from the best man. Again, ever mindful of the evil eye, the toast went something like this:

> May all your days be braced with brine,
> With vinegar and turpentine.
> The dogs will howl, your bed will creak,
> Your geese run foul, your roof will leak,
> Sticks and stones will mar your days.
> Your mother-in-law will count the ways.

The feasting, the drinking, the singing that followed can only be compared to bubbles from a glass of champagne. The gypsies, singly, moved around the table, playing each person's request. "*Ciganski Plac*" ("A Gypsy's Lament") seemed to be the favorite. To appease the unbidden guest, the eye?

After the feasting, after the gypsies, and we, the kids, had eaten, after the tables were cleared away, the dancing began, on and on, until time to eat again.

Not until the final meal was served and the dishes washed did Mama, Aunt Julie and Aunt Liza come up from the basement — Aunt Liza first. Whipping off her apron, she began:

> The world is really full of drips,
> My friend seduced my lover.
> But I'll just swing and sway my hips,
> And find myself another.

As she sang, a circle of ladies was formed — at a wedding, always a circle of ladies — and they sang, each one in turn, each song naughtier than the last. When they stopped to catch their breath, the men began — beginning with "*Ja Parobok s' Kapushan*" ("I'm a Gentlemen from Kapushan").

> I'm a gentleman from Kapushan.
> No one like me. No one. None.
> Have no wife that would deploy me.
> Have no children to annoy me.
> No one like me. No one. None.
> I'm a gentleman from Kapushan.

A wife would want a flour bin,
> A sturdy board, a rolling pin.
> She'd want an apron, trim and neat.
> Little slippers for her feet.
> No, no, I'm having too much fun.
> I'm a gentleman from Kapushan.

> A wife would want a flower bed,
> A silken kerchief for her head.
> While I, a flick for come-what-may,
> My work is finished for the day.
> No, no, my life has just begun:
> I'm a gentleman from Kapushan.

Another sang:

> Madam with your arms akimbo,
> Let me stand beneath your window.
> Serenade you tenderly,
> Your every dream will be of me.

And still another:

> On yonder hill there is a bracken.
> In your eyes a certain lackin'.
> You won't say "yes," and you won't say "no."
> Madam will you let me go?

Then back to the ladies, a nice respite for the musicians, who had been playing since dawn. A little rest before the Bridal Dance.

Because the Bridal Dance is still observed, may I explain? Actually it's the Bartering of the Bride, during which one pays to dance with her, a custom harkening back to a tribal time when "her" people would not let the bride go, crying "*Yeschche nasha*" (she is still ours) until "his" people had paid enough. Ena's wedding had reached that point.

The room was cleared, the bridesmaids encircled the bride and the people lined up to dance. The cake was cut, the whiskey poured, and Aunt Liza and Aunt Julie, Aunt Julie with apron wide open where money was to be dropped, were set to sing:

> *Redovi* (the wedding dance) is now begun.
> Each intruder must be gone,
> Every wagging tongue must cease,
> Must forever hold its peace.

Adding, after each drop of a coin, "*Yeschche nasha.*"

The dance progressed, and the singing, mindful of the "eye," went something like this:

> Our bride, how did she grow so fair,
> Mud from boots up to her hair.
>
> Her face is like a pretty picture,
> But from her mouth, oh, what a lecture.
>
> She'll never bake a loaf of bread.
> Our bride would rather stay in bed.
>
> Our groom, that coat, he'll have to hock it.
> Not a penny in his pocket.
>
> What's this? Another problem looms.
> A bridesmaid's eye is on the groom.
>
> No problem there we can't abide.
> The best man's eye is on the bride.
>
> The bridegroom pleads, please, just one kiss.
> No, no, she cried. No. None of this.

The last to dance were relatives: Aunt Julie and Uncle Maksim, Aunt Liza and Uncle Jakub, relatives from Sharon, Little Julie, Little Liza, me.

When that part comes, the tenor of the verses changes. No more Evil Eye.

> Angels up in Heaven chant.
> The bride is dancing with her aunt.

Or uncle, or cousin, as the case may be, each verse ending with:

> But when the groom reclaims his bride,
> Even angels step aside.

The last of the relatives to dance was Mama, whose duty it was to remove Ena's veil, the cue for Michael to dash in, and if he managed to knock down a few people, so much the better. With a grand flourish from the gypsies and cries of happiness from all present, the groom swept Ena off her feet and away they went. A few more dances to tie things up, and the wedding was over. The ladies fell into cleaning up, the men putting the furniture back into place.

I washed the kids and we went to bed, and even though I was lying there, my body was still full of music, still swinging and swaying to the tune of violins.

The next day, the house was again merry with friends and relatives. There was plenty of food and drink. It was the custom on the second day for the men to throw coins mixed with dirt on the floor for the bride to sweep up to test her housekeeping.

"There, you missed some," was the cry as more and more coins were thrown into a spot already swept up. "What sort of housekeeper will you be?"

Before the end of the week, Ena and Michael left for Sharon, Pennsylvania, where Michael worked in a steel mill. Tears all over again. After that, everything fell into place again: Pap and the men off to work in the morning, Mama with her chores, and I back to school, running errands and minding the kids.

One evening, watching Mama making noodles for the evening meal, I asked, "Mama? Someday, will you show me how to make noodles?"

A Basketful of Things

On any day, if the first person to cross your threshold is a woman, you'll have bad luck all day. Big bad luck if a lady, little bad luck if a little girl. And that was the truth. Even Uncle Mike said that was the truth. And, if this happened on any of three main holy days — the day before, the very day, and the day after Easter, Christmas or New Year's — you'll have bad luck for the WHOLE YEAR. That's why Mama was crying.

That's why on these days, all the little boys were up before dawn, running around to all the houses, pounding on the door:

> Wake up, wake up, and let me in.
> Or wolves will blow your whole house in.
> Your crops will blight,
> Your hens take flight,
> And thieves will enter through the night.

Mikie had been practicing all week. And the ladies, already waiting, already up because of so much to do, were ready to throw open their doors and sing:

> Come in, come in, bright harbinger,
> Of cheer, good will. Gay arbiter.
> Already, now, my morning hums.
> Come, fill your hands with sugar plums.

In every house, the boys got something, and the first one in got the most and the best. That's why the trouble started.

Mama *told* our Mikie to go first to Aunt Julie's house, but he wanted to be first in all the houses, first Aunt Liza's, then to all the others and by the time he got to Aunt Julie's house, Aunt Liza had already been there to borrow something.

But it wasn't Aunt Liza's fault. Aunt Liza thought Mikie had already been there. "Mikie was at my house an hour ago. Wasn't any boy here?"

Maybe the boys just didn't want to go to Aunt Julie's. She was always hollering at them for going through her yard, but Mikie should have gone there first, and now he was crying, ". . . and she didn't give me anything. Just slammed the door in my face."

After breakfast, Mama asked me to run up to Aunt Julie's. "Tell her we need some sugar. Here's a cup. Then tell me what she says. Run."

Mama didn't have to tell me to run. And I knew very well Mama didn't need any sugar. We had lots of it, but something had to be done, anything, so as not to spoil our Easter. After all the scrubbing and cleaning. And all that baking! Already Mama had the Easter basket on the table, ready to fill up to take to church. Now this. *I'll tell Aunt Julie we really need some sugar.*

But when I got to Aunt Julie's gate, I heard loud voices, like hollering. And people in the yard.

First it sounded like Aunt Julie, then like Aunt Liza, then like both. Aunt Liza was standing on her porch shouting up at Aunt Julie, and Aunt Julie was standing on her upstairs porch shouting down at Aunt Liza.

"You did, you did. On purpose you did. You and Marja."

Marja? That was Mama.

"Why would I do that? Why would Marja?" said Aunt Liza.

"So I have bad luck. All year. Because you don't like me. You and Marja. I know. I know everything. That's why my pascha fell flat." She was holding some flattened dough in her hand.

"Your pascha fall flat because you slam door. So hard I think my pascha fall too. It's your temper," reasoned Aunt Liza.

"Oh, now I have a temper. And you, Missis Sugarmouth? What do you have? Ha. I know you.

"Remember last week? Again you come early. All day I wear my dress inside out so nothing happen. Stayed barefoot. Now I have a temper."

"Oh, Julie, that Ole Country stuff. Barefoot all day. Even Marja say, 'That Julie, she too much Ole Country.'"

"Oh, even Marja say. Marja with her shoes on. Marja, the Amerikanka. My, my, my. Back in the Old Country she jumped from cow dung to cow dung to keep her feet from freezing, and now — what a fine lady. Turds on her. As for my brother . . . ."

"Julie, stop it. People hear."

"I'll not stop. He, too, forget Old Country, forget how I took care of him. Our mother away sometime two weeks, working, and he so sick. 'Julie, water, Julie, water,' he cried. Two candles I burned so he wouldn't die. How fast we forget. Tell him, dear Lizka, please, for me… ."

"Julie, stop it."

"Tell him, I would rather a stranger dropped his filth on my doorstep than for him or his family to even cross my threshold. As for you, Lizka dear..."

But Aunt Liza had already dashed into her kitchen, and came out holding two large pans over her head. "And for me, dear Julka, what?" she cried.

"For you dear Lizka — "

That was as far as she got. Aunt Liza began making such a din with the two pans, banging them together, then against the pump handle, then against the house, back together again, that I had to put my hands over my ears. Every time Aunt Julie opened her mouth, Aunt Liza began all over again, this time even smacking herself against the pump handle, first one side, then the other, then all over again until Aunt Julie just had to stop.

"What for me, dear Julka? I think I no hear you. So much noise here. What for me?"

Then nothing, just Aunt Julie looking down on Aunt Liza, and Aunt Liza, holding two pans high over her head, looking up at Aunt Julie. But you could feel that something was going to happen. And it did.

Very slowly, and very clearly, so everybody could hear, Aunt Julie said, "I quit. I no match for you. If I try for hundred years, I no match. So, dear Lizka, I bow to you." With these words, Aunt Julie spun around, and with her back to Aunt Liza, she threw up her skirts and bowed, and *she had no underwear on.*

I ran all the way down the street, through Donelko's yard, down the alley, and didn't stop until I was in our kitchen. Mama had already taken the pascha out of the oven, admiring, and Uncle Mike watching.

"Annie, I was beginning to worry. What happened? Where's the sugar?"

"I c—can't t—tell you," I said stammering.

"Tell me. What did Aunt Julie say?"

"N—no. I m—mean y—yes." I glanced at Uncle Mike and continued, "I c—can't t—tell you."

"Come into the bedroom, then," said Mama. There I told her everything. "*O, Hospodi,*" she breathed.

When she returned to the kitchen she told Uncle Mike everything, in Hungarian, so I wouldn't be embarrassed. Uncle Mike said nothing. Uncle Fedor laughed.

But Mama didn't think it was funny. "What shall we do?"

"Nothing," said Uncle Mike. "They get over."

"When? Today? Tomorrow, Easter."

"You see. Finish baking."

Mama was making the last of her little cakes, the apricot and the cottage cheese, when Little Julie stepped into the kitchen, holding onto a small basket.

"Mama said to give you your things," she said, placing the basket on the table, then stepping back to the door as if she were afraid.

"What things?"

"What she borrowed."

Mama went through the basket. "Did she have to give them back right now? Today?" She took out a can of sardines, a bar of Sweetheart soap, some salt.

"Salt? Nobody gives back salt. And an egg. Nobody gives back an egg."

Looking further she brought out an empty spool of thread that promptly rolled out of her hand and under the table, Little Julie and I after it. Under the table we looked at each other.

We got out from under the table.

I placed the spool on the table. Little Julie backed up to the door. "Mama said for me to hurry."

"Here, Julka," said Mama. "A cookie."

"Mama said don't take nothing."

"Okay, but you come back. Tonight you come back. Ask your Mama."

"Okay." She picked up her basket and ran out of the door so fast she almost tripped.

The first thing Mama did was pick up the salt and throw it on the stove, where it burst into a little flame and died. "I neither no want bad luck. Even egg she return."

Nobody really returned an egg. That was so if you changed your mind about being mad you could go back the next day with the egg. It meant making up. "*An obnovlene*," Uncle Mike said. Now Aunt Julie owed us nothing. Now she had no reason to ever come to our house.

And that's what Mama was crying about: That Aunt Julie would never come to our house any more. Uncle Mike was pacing the floor, holding his pipe, thinking on what to say.

"The old people were right," he began. "A woman in the morning means trouble. As it was in the beginning, so to the end. In the morning a woman means trouble."

"For once," said Uncle Fedor, "I agree with you. A woman is never good in the morning. Only at night."

Uncle Mike frowned at Uncle Fedor, then turned to Mama again. "Marcha, sometimes one must hold a candle to Lucifer."

"How many candles must I hold for him?" cried Mama.

Later I asked Uncle Mike, "Who is Lucifer?" and he told me.

Story of Lucifer

Before there was an Earth, there was only a Heaven. Only God and His angels. All beautiful. But there was one angel more beautiful than all the others — one called the Morning Star, named Lucifer.

Lucifer was not only the most beautiful of God's angels — he was also God's favorite. And that is where the problem began.

Lucifer became very vain. Also, very jealous. To be the Morning Star was not enough for Lucifer. He wanted to be Master of the Universe. He wanted to be God.

Lucifer had no trouble in bringing angels to his side. He did have a certain amount of power. First he flattered. Then he planted seeds of discontent. He promised favors. In no time there was a war — erupting with such a BANG, every star in the universe went flying helter-skelter. New planets were born. Among them, the planet Earth.

Lucifer never lost his power. Driven out of Heaven, he began to rule out of a netherworld, from where, to this day, he continues to battle against God. No sooner God implants a seed of love and beauty into one of His creatures, Lucifer comes right in and drops a seed of jealousy.

"That," continued Uncle Mike, "is how Eve lost paradise. Disguised as a serpent, Lucifer sneaked into the Garden of Eden. He got nowhere with Adam, but Eve was easy. All he did was flatter her.

"And that is why, to this day, a woman is not to be trusted in the morning. And that is the reason for this trouble between your Aunt Julie and Aunt Liza. Jealousy. And it's Lucifer who is doing it."

"Why do they let him?" I cried.

"Because he is smooth. He could even do it to you. Anything to make your mother angry.

"He won't do it any more. I'll punch him right in the nose."

"No-no-no-no-no," said Uncle Mike. "God still loves him. Lucifer is still His Morning Star. But Lucifer is afraid of the light, afraid to be exposed. That is why sometimes we must hold a candle to him."

And that is why Mama was crying, "How many times must I hold that candle?"

And why Uncle Mike was saying, "*March, Marcha*. Many, many times."

When Pap came home, Uncle Mike told him everything. He listened, said nothing, went outside to the woodshed. When he returned, he said to me, "Annie, run to Aunt Julie's. Tell her we need . . . . Mama, what we need?"

"Nothing. We need nothing."

"Everybody need something."

"Nothing." Mama was crying again. "Not even Easter I need."

But something had to be done. Pap turned to me. "Annie, go to Aunt Julie's. Tell her we need one egg."

"But we have one egg. Aunt Julie just returned…"

"We need another egg."

I went. Nobody wanted Aunt Julie mad. Not at Eastertime. After all that rosary, after all that standing in church on Monday, Wednesday, and Friday evenings. Why did Aunt Julie and Aunt Liza have to argue?

Pap was right. We have to borrow an egg. But why me? He knows that Aunt Julie doesn't like me. Ever since I wrote that letter to Father Sandor about all the ladies gossiping — that they came to our house every Wednesday and Friday evening, said the rosary, then sat around the rest of the evening and gossiped. Even Gavaj said that, sitting upstairs in his room and listening.

Father Sandor gave the letter to Uncle Maksim. Uncle Maksim gave it to Aunt Julie, and she brought it right down to our house and threw the letter on the table.

"*Skaranje*" (a wickedness), said Aunt Julie. "Nine letters she wrote."

It wasn't nine letters; it was nine pages. Today I'd give anything to know what it was I had written. Nine pages! I never saw Aunt Julie so angry.

"You're nothing but a dirty little troublemaker," she shouted at me.

I shouted right back, "And you're a dirty BIG trouble-maker. Everybody knows that." And I didn't stammer.

At once I told her I was sorry, and now, here I am, standing at Aunt Julie's gate, afraid to go in. Soon, I saw Little Julie come out on their porch. I waved for her to come down.

She did.

"What's your mother doing, Julie?"

"She's crying."

"Mine, too."

We stood there looking at each other, at the gate, at the yard, saying nothing. Glancing down toward Aunt Liza's house, I saw Little Liza at their window, looking up at us.

"Look. Lizka. Let's call her." Without waiting for an answer, I waved for her to come up.

Almost at once she was running up the alley and through Aunt Julie's yard.

"What's your mother doing, Lizka?"

"She's crying. Real hard."

"Mine, too."

"And mine. What shall we do?"

"I don't know. Pap said to borrow an egg."

"An egg?"

"Yes," I said to Little Julie. "From your mother."

"But we just gave you an egg."

"I know. Maybe we should go to Aunt Liza's first. Julie, you go to Aunt Liza's and say your mother needs an egg."

"But my mother didn't say that."

"I know your mother didn't say that. Can't you even pretend? Do you want your mother to cry all day, and all Easter Sunday, and Easter Monday? And Easter Tuesday? Just say your m—mother needs an egg."

She went.

In a little while she was back, an egg in one hand and a cookie in the other. "She gave me a cookie, too. See?"

"I told you it was easy. Now you, Lizka. You go to Aunt Julie's. Say, 'my Mama needs an egg.'"

"Okay." Little Lizka wasn't afraid of anything. In a little while, she too came back with an egg. Now it was up to me. "Lizka, what did Aunt Julie say?"

"Nothing."

Maybe Aunt Julie would say nothing to me, just give me an egg, but when she opened the door and saw it was me, she hollered, "What do you want here?"

"An e—egg. Mama needs an e—egg."

She was looking past me down the stairs and there were Lizka and Julka, looking up at us.

"So. A monkey yet you make from me. Go away," she shrieked.

I ran down the steps, almost knocking Little Julie over, who was running up the steps and wiping her hands over the front of her dress, egg all over her fingers. When I leaped onto the porch, there was another egg splattered all over Aunt Julie's clean porch and Little Lizka running down the alley.

I ran, too, all the way home and straight into our woodshed. Those splattered eggs. *Mama was right.* I wished Easter would never happen again. I wished the whole world would never happen again.

But the world didn't end. Through a crack in the door I saw Aunt Julie pushing through our gate, dragging Little Julie behind her.

Then I heard shouts, first Aunt Julie, then Pap, then both. Then nothing.

Soon I saw Pap and Aunt Julie coming out of the house. Pap was talking nicely, gesturing for Aunt Julie to shush up. Together they went up to Aunt Julie's house.

I found a spot in the corner of the woodshed and curled up to die. If I squeezed my eyes shut tight and held my breath, maybe by morning I'd be dead. Would they be sorry.

My funeral was almost over, everybody crying, Aunt Julie, too, because it was her fault, when I heard Pap knocking at the door. "It's all right, Annie. You can come out now."

"Okay." I lifted myself off the floor and walked toward the door. Pap patted me on the head, and together we walked to the house.

Inside, the men were already seated at the table, talking, and nobody hollered at me. The kids shouted, "Annie's here, Annie's here." The Easter basket, covered with Mama's embroidered *chlebovka*, was resting on the sideboard. The good smell of Easter was everywhere. So was the excitement.

Next morning, up before dawn, our clothes already laid out. Mary and I had new dresses, Mikie a new shirt and tie, and for everybody, new shoes.

After a cup of hot tea, we headed off to church, Pap carrying the Easter basket. After church, he carried it back home again. I don't know which was more exciting, the priest when he raised the monstrance three times, crying, "*Christos Voskres!*" or Mama when she uncovered the Easter basket. "*Christos Voskres!*" she cried.

After we ate, Uncle Fedor brought down his fiddle and Pap danced, first with Mama, then with all of us. Later, when Aunt Liza and Aunt Julie and the rest came down, everybody danced and everybody sang:

Gypsy fiddles add your glory
To the Resurrection story.
Swing a little brown-eyed girl,
Give the older one a whirl.
Though dark the night, and low His Head,
Christ has risen from the dead.

On until dark. Then to bed. Because the next day was even better than the first.

On the second day of Easter, the men dowsed the ladies with water: first a little on the hands with a "*Christos Voskres*," a second time on the hands with a "*Christos Voskres*," and then a third time, POW, "*CHRISTOS VOSKRES!*" right in the face.

Aunt Liza and Aunt Julie

When I recall the evenings, they still come back like benedictions. During dishes, while Mama washed and Pap dried and the men sat around on benches, Mikie, Mary and I stood in a row before Pap and recited in proper order: Heavenly King, the Our Father, Lord Have Mercy on Us, the I Believe, and if there was a guest present (which was often — somebody looking for work), we sang "Holy God" all the way through. Then, still in line, we went to each boarder, then to the guest, bowed and kissed each person's hand, after which we sat down. Pap's "Amen" meant "Now we can talk." And talk they did. And, despite the ever-present friction between them, when Aunt Julie and Aunt Liza were there, it was even better.

Here, may I interject. It was easy to love Aunt Liza. She was always laughing and joking — ready at any point to burst into song. She was also the pretty one — an advantage in life, I was beginning to see, that had no peer. Aunt Julie, on the other hand, was big and ungainly. Not a tune in her body, tending always to feel sorry for herself. But she was there when there was work to be done.

Looking back from the vantage point of years, I find my sight considerably improved.

There is a flip side to life often unfairly addressed. Living in the background, it doesn't shine. Neither does it dance, nor does it sing. It simply does. A case in point is found in the Bible: The story of Mary and Martha. And that is where ungainly Aunt Julie stood: in Martha's shoes.

But Jesus didn't know that. As we didn't know. A little praise.

Now, a second while I extricate myself: back to where I was — to a simpler time, when life was good. And if you did something bad, all you had to do was go to Confession.

Evenings were for talking — the talk, invariably of the Old Country. Over there, everything was green. Here, all soot and grime.

"Here, summer or winter, rain or shine, to work," said Uncle Fedor once. "Over there, when it rained, we rested. When wintertime came, the work was done. All a man had to do was tend to the livestock."

"Ha," Aunt Julie bridled. "One cow. But women worked. Summer AND winter."

"So?" countered Uncle Fedor. "What work did a woman have? Sew. What kind of work is that?"

Aunt Julie bristled. "You ask what kind? Before a woman could make a shirt she had to weave the cloth. Before she could weave the cloth, she had to spin the thread. Before she could spin, the flax had to be combed. And before the flax was combed, it had to be wetted down and beaten.

"And when the shirt became so dirty you couldn't tell it from the hind end of a pig, who took the shirt to the river to beat the [bad word] out of it?"

"You're right, Julka," agreed Aunt Liza. "All men did was pester the women. When harvest came, so did the babies. But we sang." And away she started, swinging her hips:

> To the sun that awakens the sleeping sod,
> To the rain that makes things grow.
> To hands that tend to the tendrils, so,
> Then garner the harvest,
> Then garner the harvest.
>
> To hands that work the flaxen mold,
> That spin the thread to gold.
> That weave the cloth, that makes the coat,
> So Jan can a-wooing go, go, go,
> So Jan can a-wooing go.

When Aunt Liza was there, there was always singing. If only Aunt Julie could be a little nice to her. Maybe it was because Aunt Liza was the pretty one. Or maybe it was because she could make people laugh.

"Or maybe it's because Aunt Julie is unhappy with herself," Uncle Mike once said.

Often when one came, the other stayed away and Mama had to listen to both sides.

Aunt Julie was Pap's sister, which is why he defended her. "She's not the worst woman in the world."

Aunt Liza was on Mama's side. She didn't even look like she came from the Old Country. When the Arabian lady came, for Mama and the others, she brought useful stuff like dress goods, and socks for men, but for Aunt Liza there was always a ready-made blouse, a pretty scarf. Once even a necklace. The Jewish peddler brought her peppermint sticks. Everybody liked her. Until one day, matters went too far. Because of Big George. Sometimes Aunt Liza came down alone. And when she left, Big George followed her.

"Talk to her, Marja," said Uncle Mike to Mama.

"Yes, talk to her," added Aunt Julie. "If that had been me, a stone I'd get. For Liza a star."

Uncle Maksim, without looking at her, said, "But it wasn't you."

Even I felt the hurt in Aunt Julie's face. I began to defend her. They all thought I didn't know anything, but I did. "Yeah. Once I s— saw A—Aunt Liza . . . ." I began. At once Pap stopped me.

"Enough," he said. "Time for bed. Take the little ones."

I did, and he followed me up. To tell me to keep my mouth shut, I knew.

"Don't tell everything you see," he said. "People make trouble from nothing."

I knew that. Like the time Little Lizka and I found some face powder in Aunt Liza's bureau drawer. We put some on our faces and when we heard Aunt Liza come, we ran, and when I got home, Mama asked, "What's that on your face?" If Aunt Julie hadn't been there, I would have made something up.

"W—we f—found it o—on Aunt L—Liza's bureau." That started everything.

"Aha," cried Aunt Julie. "Now it come out. Our pretty lady: she paint her face."

I knew what that meant. Only bad ladies painted their faces.

Next day, all the men were teasing Uncle Jakub.

"Maybe your Liza hev boy fren? Yes?"

If only the men hadn't teased Uncle Jakub. When he came home from work, he went straight into the bedroom, grabbed everything from the bureau top, statues and all, and threw everything every which way. Little Liza got hit by St. Joseph. She was on the floor playing. Aunt Liza brought her screaming to our house, blood all over.

After Mama cleaned her face, we all sat down and had tea, and when Uncle Jakub came after them, they all went home.

"Why do they do that?" I asked.

"Oh, Annie," said Uncle Fedor. "It's love."

Love? What did they know of love? They couldn't even read.

But I did so see Aunt Liza. Georgie Donelko and I were playing hide-and-go-seek and she was there with Big George behind our woodshed, he reaching for her. She backing away. When they saw us, Big George said, "Get out of here," and we did.

And I didn't say anything. It was Georgie Donelko who told his mother, and his mother told his father, and his father told the men at work. And that's why Aunt Liza came flying into our kitchen: no shoes, no shawl.

"Now what did you do?" asked Mama.

"Nothing. I did nothing wrong. *Vera Bohu.*"

"You must have done something. Here, sit down. Have some tea. He'll come for you."

But he didn't. When we went to bed, she and Mama were still having tea, and when we got up the next morning, she was still there.

When Uncle Mike came home from the night shift, he asked, "Now what did you do?" Because he was older, he could scold her and he often did.

Again, she said, "Nothing. Just talking. What is wrong with just talking?"

Uncle Mike looked hard at Aunt Liza then went to the wash basin to wash up. After he had dried himself he said to Aunt Liza, "Go home. Everything will be all right. Sleep erases. Go home."

After she left, Uncle Mike sat down to eat. "Too many men," he said. "Not enough women. Marja, talk to her."

"That's the problem. Too much talk." The baby began to cry.

"Maybe she needs another baby," Uncle Mike said.

Uncle Mike had already gone upstairs to sleep when the door flew open. Aunt Liza. Dripping wet.

"What happened?" cried Mama.

"What happened? Look what happened." Aunt Liza lifted her skirt to show a long, bloody gash on her leg.

"Liza! Did Jakub . . .?"

"No. Climbing through the cellar window."

"Why . . .?"

"Because the door was locked. I had to break the cellar window."

After Mama had washed off the blood, the cut didn't look too bad. After Aunt Liza had changed into dry clothes, Mama asked, "Now tell me. Why are you wet?"

"That *chort* [devil]. First I crawled through the window. Didn't hear a thing. I tip-toed up the stairs. Still nothing. But when I saw the bedroom door closed shut I got scared. Maybe he was dead. Slowly I opened the door and all at once I AM DROWNING. He had a bucket of water over the door. There I was, dripping wet, and there he was asleep on my *perina* [feather tick], an empty whiskey bottle beside him. Lizka in the next room didn't even wake up. Or maybe she was too scared. I picked up the bottle, cracked it on his head and ran."

"What if you hurt him?"

"I hope I killed him."

That's when the door opened. It was Little Liza.

"Mama, come home. Papa said to come. He said to tell you he'll never drink again."

Aunt Julie and Elsa

Aunt Julie could be nice, too. When she baked something good she always brought Mama a taste. And when Mama wasn't feeling well, it was she who came to help. Then she'd say, "See. I come. Do Liza come? Never."

What could Mama say? What she said was true.

But come evenings, it was Aunt Liza who made everyone laugh. It was she who knew all the songs. Aunt Julie couldn't sing a note. When she tried, Uncle Maksim laughed. "You sound like a frog," he once said.

But she made the best bread and rolls and cakes. One evening she and Uncle Maksim and Little Julie came early; Aunt Julie had just finished making some cold cakes, a recipe she got from the Braddock ladies. Mama was holding the platter, admiring the new cakes, Aunt Julie was looking at Uncle Maksim to see if he would say something. You could tell he was proud but, no, he didn't say a word. That's when Aunt Liza dashed in.

"I have something to tell you," she cried.

All eyes were now turned toward Aunt Liza.

Mama, still holding the platter of cakes, said, "I know. You're pregnant."

"How did you know?"

"I know the look," she said, placing the cakes on the table, where they stayed the rest of the evening like poor rejected souls. Uncle Fedor, a pretended glass of wine raised high, was already proposing a toast. "To a boy," he cried.

"A boy, a boy," was the cry from the other men.

"Enough, already," said Pap.

When all had gone home, Uncle Mike said, "Again, for Julie, nothing."

I always had the feeling that something wasn't right at Aunt Julie's house. "If Julie had a son, big and strong like her," Uncle Mike once said, "Maksim would have forgiven her for growing into such a big woman. He would have been proud of a big son. But all she produced was a girl."

She was big all right. Even her voice was big. When she talked it sounded like hollering. Once I asked, "Why is Aunt Julie so big, and Uncle Maksim so little?"

"That happens," said Mama. "When Uncle Maksim married Aunt Julie, she was tiny. Not yet fifteen. Not yet finished growing. Not until after they were married did she begin to grow."

Just the same, Aunt Julie was always trying to please him. Always, it was, "My Maksim this, my Maksim that." Once something happened that almost put a change to this: a letter from Uncle Maksim's mother.

Letters from the Old Country all started the same way. First, "Praised be God." Then a full page of greetings, first from all of them, then to all of us, then the news. But this letter skipped all that.

"*Drahi* Maksim," Gavaj read. "I write about your sister. She wants to marry, and the boy wants to marry her, but he is from a rich family. His parents do not want our Elsa. The two hide to meet. Maksim, for God's sake, send passage money for America before she brings shame on all our families. Julka, *draha*, you, too, I ask."

At once, Aunt Julie said, "Yes. We will send money." Then added, looking at Uncle Maksim for a nod, "We will put a cot in the kitchen."

That's how Elsa came to America.

And Aunt Julie was very proud of her. Elsa was prettier than even Aunt Liza; made Aunt Julie proud. She basked in Elsa's presence. Every Sunday somebody came searching for a bride, and every Sunday Elsa would hide —-anywhere — in the outside toilet — until they left.

Soon, nobody came, and Aunt Julie was becoming worried. Her chance to play mother-of-the-bride was going down the drain. Her chance of getting the passage money back was also going down the drain.

"What does she want?" she said to Mama once.

One day Jaran Segin, a young widower, came inquiring. He had been working and saving money to bring his wife to America, but she died before she had a chance to come. When Jaran came inquiring, Aunt Julie's hopes soared again.

"He will pay your passage debt. You will have a good life," she kept saying to Elsa. She pleaded with Uncle Maksim. "Talk to her. She is your sister."

Even Mama pushed.

What could Elsa do? The wedding was arranged. But on her wedding night, Elsa jumped out of the window. Mama heard her crying outside our gate. But it was too late. Everybody said that. Even the priest. He reminded her of her promise before the Blessed Altar and what that meant: that marriage was a holy sacrament, and if she refused to live with her husband, she'd have a mortal sin and burn in hell.

Mama began to say, "What will you do? Where can you go? Back to the Old Country?"

"Jaran isn't the worst man in the world," said Pap.

So, Elsa went to live with Jaran.

But that didn't make matters right. At church, Elsa sat beside her husband, but she didn't pray. And when they came to our house, she didn't open her mouth. Mr. Segin began coming down alone.

"All night she cry," he said. What had begun for Aunt Julie as an asset turned bleakly negative. Uncle Maksim began to blame her. "You wanted the passage money," he shouted one day. "You couldn't wait. Now I can't stand looking at you. Better if she had died."

One day Aunt Julie said to Mama, "My life, too, is over."

But Uncle Mike was optimistic. "The Segins will make it. They're young. Like broken branches: grafted to a good tree they will bind together."

And he was right. Soon Elsa began to talk and to smile. She began to fix my hair, this way and that. One day I heard Mama tell Pap, "Elsa is with child."

Until something happened again. One morning — the men had already gone to work and Uncle Mike had just come in — a young man came knocking on our door. He said he was Stefan Koren, he was looking for Elsa, that he had written many letters but none had been answered.

That was him: the young man who loved Elsa.

But it was too late. When Uncle Mike told him what had happened, he cried, "But I asked her to wait for me. I told her I was coming." With these words, he left.

"What are we going to do?" asked Mama.

"About the letters, keep your mouth shut. Forever. About Stefan, we have to tell Elsa. I will tell her."

When Uncle Mike returned from the Segins, all he said was, "We have to pray."

This time, Elsa stopped going to church, stopped coming to our house. Mama had to go up to see her. "For the baby's sake."

One day, Uncle Maksim received a letter from the coal mines at Clymer, Pennsylvania. A young man by the name of Stefan Koren had been killed, and among his things was found one address, that of Maksim Neborak.

Father Sandor called the parish priest at Clymer, and arrangements were made for the burial. Uncle Maksim and Uncle Mike were the only ones to go. Elsa cried to go, but the trip would have been bad for her.

When my uncles returned, they said there was only the priest, the cantor and one altar boy. "He's buried now, a stranger in a strange land," said Uncle Mike.

Elsa asked for one thing: the letter from the coal company. Then she dyed all her clothing black. When the baby came, Mr. Segin made all the arrangements. Mama was the godmother, Uncle Jakub was godfather. The baby was baptized "Stefan."

"We will call him 'Stefan' if you like," Mr. Segin said to Elsa. There was no christening, just a baptism at the church.

"An orphan already," said Mama.

"But they are young," said Uncle Mike. "All will be right yet."

Again, Uncle Mike was right. Before long, there was a change in Elsa. Elsa was heard singing lullabies, laughing at the little one's antics. She gave up wearing black and began coming to our house. Everybody was glad again, even Uncle Maksim. Sometimes, watching Elsa play with little Stefan, his eyes would fill up with tears.

Still, something wasn't as it should be. The baby brought joy into their lives, but the joy wasn't shared. Once, Mr. Segin said, "Yes, she is happy at last. Because of little Stefan, her other Stefan has been returned to her. Her songs and her laughter are for the one in the grave."

This time, Uncle Mike didn't like it. "The child will not be long in this world."

"God couldn't be so cruel," said Mama.

"God could be so kind," he said. And again, he was right.

Little Stefan became ill one evening. "Come at once," said Mr. Segin, and Mama went. She stayed all night, but before morning, Little Stefan was gently lifted from his mother's arms.

At the funeral, Uncle Maksim could barely keep Elsa from throwing herself into the grave. Father Sandor had to lead her away, down the hill, the people following, the ladies wailing.

That's when another cry was heard. All stopped, turned and looked up. Mr. Segin, alone, was sobbing at the grave.

Slowly, Elsa separated herself from the group — began walking back to the grave.

"We must leave now, all of us," said Father Sandor.

The succeeding years were kind to the Segins. In due time, a little girl was born, Little Elsa. Then a boy, Little Jaran, then another, Little Stevie.

But Aunt Julie's life continued to be a barren one. Uncle Maksim just couldn't or wouldn't be nice to her. In time, he stopped coming to our house, but Mama was always friendly with Aunt Julie.

One cold morning — I was on my way to school — Aunt Julie dashed into our kitchen.

"Come at once. Maksim. Maksim."

Mama went. Uncle Maksim had had a stroke.

All day and all through the night, Mama and Aunt Julie stayed with him, and it seemed, Mama said, that Uncle Maksim was trying to say something. Toward morning, he gave up and slowly slipped away.

Now, so many years later, I don't wonder about love. *Aunt Julie? Love?* Perhaps, in the end, the greatest. Hers survived on so little. Looking up at their candles, so strong, so true, I prayed: "Rest in peace, dearest Uncle and dearest Aunt, and forgive me, too, my trespasses."

The cantor is now beginning the thrice holy hymn: "*Cheruvimi, Serafimi.*" I glance toward a bank of smaller lights, looking for all the world like rows of desks in a schoolroom. I see Caroline, Margaret Jean, Elsie, Ellis and Anthony. Over to the side, flipping and flapping, Susie.

"*Cheruvimi, Serafimi,*" repeats the cantor for the second time.

Who can say that the *Cheruvimi* are not faces of all the departed past, preserved through memory after memory, through eons and eons of time to the point where trillions can dance on the point of a needle? That the songs all mankind sings are not the remembered songs from the time when man first beheld the Face of God? When discord was introduced by a jealous god?

"*Cheruvimi, Serafimi,*" sings the cantor for the third time.

The priest begins to leave the Table of Preparation. As the people sing, "invisibly escorted by angelic hosts," the gifts of bread and wine are brought to the main altar.

"Peace be with all," chants the priest.

"And with your spirit," sing the people.

Part II

Thanksgiving

By the time I had reached the fifth grade, I had learned a good bit. Pap thought I was the smartest. He never said as much, but I knew. The kids liked me, too, but once out of the house I walked alone; I was never a part of that clutch of girls who giggled and laughed their way to and from school. And in school, I still sat in the back row. I think it was because of the stammer. But I could read; the people in the books became my friends.

I liked the Jane and Dick stories. Their mother didn't even look like a mother, always nicely dressed in a white apron, new shoes, her hair done up in a knot, and their house so neat. When they sat down to eat, they passed the food around and said "please" and "thank you." I tried to teach our Mary and Mikie to say "please" and "thank you" and not to eat so fast, but Uncle Fedor said, "Eat fast. If you don't, a *zobrak* [beggar] will come along and clean up your plate."

It was like living in two worlds, home and then school. And I liked them both; I liked the songs we sang at home, and I liked the songs we sang in school; I liked the stories about the Old Country, and I liked the stories about the New Country. I liked the one about the First Thanksgiving, about how the Pilgrims, finally having a good harvest, decided on a Thanksgiving feast and decided to invite the Indians.

". . . and for the first meal," Miss Wilkins was telling us, "there was wild turkey stuffed with chestnuts, mounds of cornbread and potatoes, Indian pudding and cranberries. For dessert, huge slabs of pumpkin pies. What are your mothers making?" she asked the class. Hands shot up.

"Mincemeat pie," said Ellen.

"Apple and pumpkin," said Eleanor.

I just listened. Mama didn't even know what a pie was. Neither did I. All Mama made was *kolachki*, but on Thanksgiving Day, she didn't even do that. On Thanksgiving Day we butchered the pig. That was because all the men were home on that day.

The day before Thanksgiving, by the time I got home from school, Mama already had the pork barrel scrubbed and scalded, the meat grinder ready, pans and trays all washed and drying on the porch, because by next morning, at crack of dawn, all the men had to be at their places in the yard in case something went wrong. Sometimes the pig got away.

Before I was up, Mama had the rice pudding made. When I awakened, then the kids, it was my job to feed them, then keep them out of the way. Parts of the pig were already beginning to come in: the heart, the liver, kidneys and things. Some of these were chopped up with garlic and hot pepper, then placed into an iron skillet to simmer at the back of the stove, to be poured over rice for the evening meal. The rest was put aside for sausage.

After this came the bigger pieces from which the fat was trimmed off, then thrown into a pot for rendering. By the end of the day, the pot was full of lard, to be poured into a huge crock. What was left was cracklins.

The cracklins were kept on a lower pantry shelf for as long as they lasted: delicious eaten by the handful, great with scrambled eggs, and out-of-this-world when mashed into potatoes. There was never enough. Always, Pap would say, "Next year we'll have to kill two pigs."

The big pieces of meat were separated, some for smoking, some to be preserved in the lard, and some cut into huge slabs of bacon, to be salted, covered with red paprika, then stored in the cold cellar for winter snacking. I can still see Uncle Mike bringing a piece of bacon up from the cellar, placing it on a cutting board, taking out his penknife, testing it for sharpness, then neatly and slowly, cutting away a little slice, looking at it, then sliding it onto his tongue, rolling it around a bit, chewing a little, then swinging around and pointing his knife at me. "And when the *Starosta* (marriage broker) comes looking for you," he would tease, "we'll bring out the bacon."

Marry? Me? What would Mama do?

When time came to make the kolbassi, I helped. All leftover meat was chopped up, salted and spiced. It was my job to clean the casings. With the dull side of a table knife, I scraped away bits of fat, blew into the casing to see how clean it was coming, scraped some more, carefully so as not to tear it, blow and scrape, until all the casings were "as clean as window glass," said Mama.

"See, Uncle Mike," I would say.

And again he teased, "Now you can get married."

When the sausage was done, the work was about completed. Pap carried the meat down into the cold cellar, then outside again, because —Uncle Mike was already roasting the pig's feet, the tail and the ears, already singing:

> When I was young and in my prime,
> I fed on dew and turpentine,
> But now that I am old and bent,
> A little tea, and I'm content.

then turning to Mikie —

> But you, because you're not so big,
> For you a little tail of pig.

Because he was a boy, he got the tail. Mary and I got the ears. Mama, waiting with a pot, got the pig's feet.

"For Sunday," she would say. All day Saturday the pig's feet would be simmering at the back of the stove until all the meat fell off the bones. The amber liquid was then strained into bowls, the meat plopped into the center, then left on the table in the cold pantry to gel for Sunday's meal.

The last was the head, Uncle Mike slowly rolling it, backward and over, forward and back again, chanting softly as he turned, turning and chanting, something that sounded like *"Life is sacred. Life is good."* Uncle Fedor picking up:

> Life is short, and life is long.
> Life is like a Gypsy's song.
> One day full of joy and gladness.
> Next, a day of tears and sadness.
>
> And if the girl is not for you,
> A little glass of beer will do.

Then turning to Mikie, a little picking knife in his hand:

> And if you just so much as gander,
> Off will come your little dander.

Mikie, squealing, ducked behind me — barely noticed. We were all watching Uncle Mike, mesmerized, listening to his chant:

> Life is sacred, life is good.

All at once, at the right moment, and only he knew that, he plunged a sharp stick into an opening in the head, and lifted it. With a cry that echoed not only throughout the Hollow but backward into time, came words from a pagan past. Raising the hog's head to the skies, he cried:

> Oh, hail ye gods, who this day meet,
> The sacrifice is now complete.

With another triumphant shout, the trophy was carried into the kitchen, we after him, some of the men making the sign of the cross. Three times.

The hog's head was placed on a platter already waiting on the kitchen table. The ensuing scene is etched in my memory: The men relaxed at the table, each with his own penknife, picking out morsels of the meat while they talked, now in low tones, now joshing in disagreement. By the light of the kerosene lamp, we could see their shining faces, their darkened silhouettes, their moving shadows on the walls.

And now, as I gaze at the flickering candle lights, I see them again, sitting with the kings of Tara, at the banquet halls of Valhalla, at every gathering of ancient gods on the stormy summits of Tatra.

Monday morning, Miss Wilkins asked if everyone have enough to eat, enough turkey, enough of pumpkin pie." All cried out, "Yeah, yeah. Turkey, pie and ice cream."

What could I say? They'd probably laugh.

About Christmas

One morning in early December we were awakened to *snow*! Everywhere! It covered the black cinders along the tracks, it covered the muddy sidewalks, it covered all the garbage in the dump, the drab hillside. It etched every tree in white. *Like sugar on a licorice stick,* I thought.

Uncle Mike, who had just come in, was stomping his feet and shaking the new snow off his shoulders. "Saint Michael on a white horse," he said.

Saint Michael's Day came during the first week of December, and if snow fell on his day, that is what everyone said: "Saint Michael arrived on a white horse."

We could hardly eat our breakfast. As soon as we were bundled up, we dashed out. The boys were already throwing snowballs.

"Here Mikie. A snowball. Throw it. *Not at me.*"

Our exuberance carried into the schoolhouse — into each classroom. As soon as I had taken my place, as soon as the Twenty-Third Psalm was read, the Our Father recited, Miss Wilkins announced, "And now we will sing a Christmas carol."

> Christmas time is drawing near.
> Santa Claus will soon be here.

After the singing, Miss Wilkins made another announcement. "Today we are going to write letters to Santa."

"Anything we want?" asked Ellis Boyd.

"Anything."

"Anything," she said. I began to write, snatching at every item that danced through my head. A wagon for Mikie. Two. A sled. Two. A doll for Mary. Two. Storybooks, crayons, gloves, mittens, scarves. A sweater for Pap. Two. A blouse for Mama. Two. Two of everything. Then for me: a blue silk dress and a pink silk dress.

On the board was the address:

> SANTA CLAUS
> NORTH POLE

Each letter was dropped into a basket on Miss Wilkins' desk. Would Mama be surprised on Christmas morning! I could hardly keep from telling her.

But even if I wanted to, I couldn't. There was no time. Advent was for cleaning. All curtains down, laundered and stretched; holy pictures cleaned, frames re-gilded. Doors varnished. New dresses made. New shoes bought. Sometimes I forgot about the letter.

Came the day before Christmas. So much to do. Mama was up before dawn. By the time we ran downstairs, there was a little Christmas bread cooling for us to taste. Then up and down the neighborhood, to Aunt Julie's, Aunt Liza's, the Donelkos, kids running in and out of the houses: "My mother needs some sugar," "Do you have an extra pan?" Mama always borrowed from Mrs. Murray, and when the pans were filled for baking, Mrs. Murray baked some in her oven. The last, and best, pan of rolls was for Mrs. Murray.

By Christmas Eve, everything was ready: the food cooked, the bread baked, the floor covered with straw. Christmas Eve was here.

Mary and I helped set the table, one chair extra for the stranger that may come in, then we joined the men and sang Christmas carols. Mama excused herself to feed the baby. That finished, she gave the baby to me, and by the time Pap had carried the big tureen of mushroom soup to the table, the baby was asleep.

We all sat down, but before we could eat, with a bit of honey, Mama made a cross on every forehead, saying "*Christos Razdajetsja.*" We answered, "*Slavite Jeho.*"

After the soup came *pirohi* with sauerkraut, *bobalki* with cottage cheese, a bowl of prunes. Occupying the place of honor, after the mushroom bowl had been removed, was the *krachunik*, a sweet dough, rolled out round and flat, covered with cottage cheese, sweetened with gold raisins.

The pig feet jelly shimmering on the pantry table was for the next day, the ham and kolbassi still roasting in the oven was for the next day, and the *holubki* (stuffed cabbage leaves) simmering on the back burner was for the next day. As soon as we had finished eating, we waited for Pap to say, "You can go now."

Did I mention that for Christmas the kitchen floor was covered with straw?

At once, the kids and I dove into the straw. Hidden throughout were walnuts, hazelnuts, almond nuts, and best of all, somewhere an orange for each of us, and there was never a Christmas Eve that Mama didn't say, "Never again." Somebody always got more than somebody else.

And no dishes to wash. They were left on the table because at midnight all the animals come in and clean off every plate, and that was true. When I sneaked down to put my note on the table —

DEAR SANTA,
PUT EVERYTHING ON THE TABLE,
I LOVE YOU SANTA.
THANK YOU.

ANNIE

the dishes were all cleaned up and put away. I had been worrying about that: Where would Santa put the presents? I hurried back up to bed. "You had better be sleeping or he won't come," the teacher said.

In the morning I awakened with a start. Daylight was peeping in, but nobody was up yet. Without making a sound, I tip-toed down the stairs. I knew where every creak was. Then into the kitchen, and there, on the table, was my note. *He didn't come.*

I picked up the note, folded it, then back upstairs.

What could have happened? I spelled each word correctly, I knew that. My writing was clear, even beautiful. "Beautiful," Miss Evans had said. And the address was correct. I copied it from the board. Slowly, the truth began to dawn on me. I had asked for too much. Two of everything. Next year I would ask for only one of everything.

When Pap came up shouting, "Wake up, wake up, you sleepy head," I was asleep. "It's Christmas morning," he called up.

Christmas morning was a flurry of getting ready for church, everybody bumping into everybody else. By the time we were standing, Mary, Mikie and me, in a row at the table having our tea, Mama had everything in control.

Finally, we were on our way.

"Hold Mikie's hand."

"I will, I will."

Aunt Julie was already up ahead, Aunt Liza behind her, but not the Donelkos yet. They were last on purpose, I knew, because they didn't get new shoes.

But who could see in church? Nobody looked at shoes. Everybody looked at the altars covered with golden cloths, lit with Christmas candles. Down to the side was a manger, Joseph standing behind Mary, Mary sitting down holding Baby Jesus. To the right were three Wise Men, to the back were the shepherds from the hill, and at the front, animals kneeling. And when the priest opened the Royal Doors, when he raised the monstrance, and cried, three times, to the right, to the left, then the center, *"Christos Razdajetsa,"* you felt your heart would explode.

Then came the Liturgy, interspersed regularly with "*Christos Razdajetsa*," ending with my favorite Christmas carol.

> When a bright star appeared,
> Mary knew time was near.
> Joseph found a manger, right.
> Little Jesus came that night.
>
> When Mary first beheld her Son,
> Soft, so softly, sang this song;
> Rest my Baby, little Mite,
> I have yet to sleep this night.
>
> Wait my mother, dear, please wait,
> While I go through Heaven's gate.
> I'll bring for you a feather bed,
> Bring soft pillows for your head.
>
> Oh, my Dear Beloved Son,
> You can't do that, Little One.
> Not an hour since Your Birth.
> You've just arrived upon this earth.
>
> Mother, dearest, don't you know?
> I was here eons ago.
> All the earth and all creation,
> 'Twas I who fashioned every nation.

On the way home, Susie Donelko walked with me. I could see her looking at my shoes. I had a fleeting thought: *Next year, my list will include shoes for Susie.*

When Susie came down later, I gave her extra cookies, then told her she had to leave. I had to, because we were waiting for the *Betlehemci*, the men from Bethlehem.

"Long ago," Gavaj was telling us once, "our people hadn't heard about Jesus, about how, because there was no room at the inn for Mary and Joseph, Jesus was born among animals in a manger. Our people hadn't heard that. The story was written in all the bibles, too, but our people couldn't read. That is why a group of men from Bethlehem decided to visit each family, carrying a manger with Little Jesus in it, so the people could see. That is why, to this day, the *Betlehemci* still come to every house, telling the story and singing Christmas carols.

"But not everybody believed the story. That is why the *Guba* came along — to frighten the people into believing."

But we believed. And when the knock came to the door, we accepted them. "They're here! They're here!"

I sprang to the door. Filling the doorway in long black robes and tall hats were two *Betlehemci*, holding a manger between them. Behind them, more tall hats.

"*Vitajce, vitajec*," cried Pap.

They at once began to sing "*Divnaja Novina* [Wondrous News], came into the house, and placed the manger on the table. When they had finished, the door, which had been carefully closed, burst open. In jumped the *Guba*, brandishing a wooden axe.

> Food and drink is my demand.
> At once, at once, is my command.
> If not, I'll smash,
> And I will bash
> All your pots and pans to hash.

Then, with axe still raised as if to strike, everybody properly cowed, he began to prowl, looking into every corner, and when he came to one of us, he'd strike the axe to the floor as if to chop off our toes, we squealing away from him. After this, one of the *Betlehemci* gave a short account of the birth of Christ, followed by everybody singing "Heaven and Earth join in the celebration," after which the *Guba* resumed his antics. One of the *Betlehemci* began to sing:

> Guba's life is filled with woe,
> He doesn't know his "to" from "fro,"
> Doesn't know his left from right.
> Our Guba isn't very bright.

And when he appeared to demur:

> Our Guba's life is filled with strife.
> He doesn't even have a wife,
> Has no children to console him,
> No *perina* to enfold him.
> *Segin* [unfortunate person] Guba.
> What a life.

The group never stayed too long. There was the next house and the next house and the next house. With one more carol, the manger was lifted and carried out. The Guba, heaving with sobs, was the last to leave, but not before one last swipe at the feet of the one who dared to follow too closely.

Back in school, after Christmas, Miss Evans asked, "What did you get for Christmas?" Someone said, "A doll," another "a sled," "a wagon," "a storybook." Nobody got two of anything. *Next Christmas I, too, will order only one, but for me, which shall it be? A blue silk dress, or a pink silk dress?* That was quite a few years ago, and I haven't yet been able to decide.

About Sauerkraut

nce I began to write, I didn't have to run to the Murrays for a note anymore, and when Mama needed something from the store, I didn't have to memorize anymore, repeating all the way to the store. I could write. When the time came to make sauerkraut, Mama was telling me what to get, watching over my shoulder as I wrote. As if she could read.

"Write careful," she said.

With the deliberate exasperation of one who knows to one who doesn't know, I replied, "Yes, Mama," then repeated aloud:

> 7 bushels of cabbage
> 1 box of salt

"Vrite. En two box-a . . . Pap, how you say da liff?" Mama spoke English every chance she got.

"Bay liff," said Pap.

"Bay liff," said Mama.

"Bay leaf," I repeated, setting my arm in proper writing position, the way Miss Mellon taught, for a beautifully rounded B, then for an "l" that flowed. Then, because Pap was watching, finishing with a big swirly line across the page.

"Un dat evair*ting*," said Mama, looking around. "No, *nye* evairting. Two box-a peppair. Now evairting. Two cup-a corn I hev. Rye bread I hev nuff. En tell Mist*air* Hessl*air* to fill every head hard, en iff he sen just vun soft, I vill mysel push in his face. Now run."

Mama didn't have to tell me to run. Already I could see the snow-white mound of crisp cabbage piled high on a white sheet in the corner of the kitchen. The pungent aroma already filled my nostrils. I placed the pencil behind the clock on the mantel, tucked the order into my fist, leaped over the doorstep, and was about to swing myself down over the steps when I noticed Susie Donelko standing right outside our kitchen door.

"Can I go too, Annie? Can I?"

"No, Susie." Susie always wanted to go to the store with me — a second grader. What if somebody saw us? "No, you can't," I whispered hard, right into her face, then dashed down the steps and across the yard and through the gate before Mama could see and make me take her along.

When I got to the road I glanced back; Susie was still standing there.

That's when I saw Bridget Murray coming out of their house. Bridget was in the fourth grade.

"Where you goin', Annie?" she called to me.

"I hafta go to the store. W—wanna come?" From the corner of my eye I could see Susie standing outside our kitchen door, but how could I ask her to come with me? With her flip-floppy soles, we'd never get back. To ease my conscience, I added to Bridget, "You'll hafta r—run."

"How come you hafta run?"

"Because I hafta order the cabbage. Because we're g—gonna make sauerkraut. "T—tonight," I added.

Bridget was now running with me. "Sauerkraut? How do you make sauerkraut?"

"Easy." I began to shout. When I shouted I didn't stammer. "Did you see that barrel on the porch? Twenty gallons it holds. And the slats, all scrubbed white? They are to hold the sauerkraut down. And that big stone? That goes on top of the wood slats. And the cabbage cutter? That big thing with the big sharp blades? Uncle Mike spent all day yesterday sharpening them, and tonight he's going to tramp the cabbage down, he and Uncle Fedor. Pap and the rest of the men will cut the cabbage and Uncle Mike and Uncle Fedor will tramp it down."

"Tramp it down? With their feet?"

"Sure. But first you have to throw some corn into the bottom of the barrel, then you break up a loaf of rye bread and throw that in. Then the cabbage — all mixed through with salt and bay leaves. Mama dumps a bushelful of cabbage in at a time and Uncle Mike will tramp it down, and when the cabbage juice starts to come, Mama bails it out."

"Juice?"

"Yes. I hold the pan while Mama ladles. Then she adds more cabbage, more salt, more ladling. That's how you make sauerkraut.

"When Uncle Mike is stomping, Uncle Fedor is playing his harmonica, and when the barrel is getting so full that Uncle Mike begins to hit the ceiling, Uncle Fedor goes in. But Uncle Mike can't play the harmonica. Instead, he claps his hands and so do we. Now and then Mama tucks in a red apple, one for each of us."

"How long does it take?"

"By Thanksgiving, when we kill the pig, the sauerkraut is almost done. But first you have to keep the sauerkraut in a warm place by the chimney. Every morning you have to take off the scum. Mama does all that. She lifts the stone off, then the slats. Then she cleans off all the scum. Then she rinses the slats and lays them on the sauerkraut, then the stone, then she covers the barrel with a clean, white cloth, and when the cabbage begins to taste like sauerkraut, Pap and somebody walk the barrel down the steps and into the cellar. All winter long it keeps. Can you come? When the cabbage is all cut up, Uncle Fedor will play his harmonica and we can dance.

"Ask your mother, okay?"

"Okay."

Inside, I went straight to Mr. Hessler and handed him the note.

"Annie, how many time I tell you: Do not run so fast. You will wear out your legs before you grow up."

"B—but Mama said . . . ."

"I know what Mama said. If there is just one soft she will herself push it in my face. You tell Mama, I myself picked for her the very best, with a half bushel extra. And for Thanksgiving I ask, for me, one little crock of sauerkraut."

Size 48 Big

Because I could talk in English, I was beginning to do Mama's shopping, but as always, there was Susie Donelko always wanting to go to the store with me, as if going to the store with me was a big thing. She even wanted to do my buying.

"Could I, Annie? Could I? Sometimes my mother lets me."

"No, she doesn't. When she needs something, I have to go."

Sometimes I let her go with me, but most of the time I didn't, because if I ran real fast, both ways, I got to jump rope with the kids, and if she tagged along, I was lucky to make it back home on time, so slow she was. Always falling. Those flippity-floppity shoes.

Once I asked her, "Why doesn't your father fix your shoes?"

She didn't know.

But once I was glad she came along. That was the time Uncle Fedor was going to a wedding and I had to go to Mandelblatt's to buy him underwear. *Underwear.*

"Why does he have to have new underwear?" I said. "He's not getting married." I should have known better than to talk back to Mama, especially when she was rolling dough. "Annie," she said, holding the rolling pin up in the air, "your uncle already is washing up. Go. And remember. Size 48 Big. Now run."

I backed out toward the door, looking at her face to see if she really meant what she said. She did. She was already flipping the dough up and around, slamming it with the rolling pin, then flipping it again, like she does when she's mad about something. With my hind end, I pushed the door out. *Underwear?* I'd rather die.

What if Sammy was there? Sammy Mandelblatt was in my class in school and sometimes after school he helped his father in the store. Would he laugh! Then he'd tell all the kids. "Annie buys underwear for men." *If the store was full of people, Sammy might even have to wait on me. God!*

I looked up and down the road. Nothing, just some chickens pecking away at the dirt. A dog came along and scared the chickens away. Dumb chickens. Dumb ole dog.

That's when Susie came along. My God. Susie yet. She was skipping along, swinging her arms up and down and around as if she really had a rope but she didn't. She never had a rope of her own. Always borrowing mine. "Could I, Annie? Could I?"

Now she was pretending she tripped, making exasperated motions with her face and her arms as if she really had. *How could she trip with no rope?*

Now she was jumping again, pretending again. I never saw anybody like her in my whole life. A good thing she couldn't see me. I hid behind the porch post. But *she did see me.*

"Annie," she called, turning into our yard.

Shut up, Susie, I thought. *If Mama hears you, I'll get it*. I jumped off the porch and through the yard. The last thing I needed was Susie. She'd probably want to go to Mandelblatt's with me, probably even want to— want to— . That's when it hit me. *Susie could buy the underwear*. I stopped in flight, then slowly sauntered back.

"Hi, Susie."

"Hi. Where ya going?"

"Oh-h. To the store. To Mandelblatt's."

"To Mandelblatt's? Could I go with you? Could I, Annie?"

"Hmmmmm. If you want to. You want to?"

"Sure. Sure I want to. Could I?"

"You'll have to run."

"Oh, I can run. Real fast I can run. What do you hafta buy?"

"Just some underwear. For Uncle Fedor," I added, raising my voice. We were already running. "He's going to a wedding. Far away. On a train."

"Once we went to a wedding. We got pop: orange and cherry and grape. All kinds. Then we got . . . ."

"Yeah, I know, I know. I know all about weddings. But now we have to go to Mandelblatt's to buy— to buy—." I couldn't say the word.

"Underwear," she finished for me. She must have heard.

I looked at her. Underwear didn't bother her a bit.

"I'm going to buy some candy, too, but first we have to buy the — underwear."

"Candy?"

"Yeah. Chocolate drops or Tootsie Rolls. Maybe licorice sticks. What kind do you like?"

"Oh, licorice sticks," she cried, almost falling flat on her face. Those shoes again.

"Watch yourself . . . I mean, be careful, Susie. You'll get hurt."

"Okay."

"But we have to run."

"I know."

"So don't fall."

"Okay."

"Susie, you are my very best friend."

"Yeah. I know. And I'm yours."

"Remember, Susie, yesterday? When I was eating my apple?"

"Yesterday?"

"Yeah. Remember? I gave you cobs."

"Oh, yeah. I remember."

"Today, maybe I'll give you some candy."   Again, she almost tripped. Those flippity soles of hers. But she heard me. "Licorice sticks?"

"I might."

"I'll do anything for you, Annie. I'll watch the baby."

"No. Not the baby." I'd never let *her* watch our baby.

"I'll do something else then. What do you want me to do?"

We arrived at the store. I looked inside. Sammy was there all right, helping his father. *God!*

"What can I do, Annie?"

"Can you buy something?"

"Sure. I can buy anything. Once I bought dill pickles for my mother."

Dill pickles. Did I remember the dill pickles. I wasn't around, so Susie had to run to the store. Because her mother was in the family way. Every time Mrs. Donelko was in the family way, she had to have *dill pickles*, but by the time Susie came home, her mother didn't want them any more.

"Take them away," she screeched, "before I throw up."

So the Donelko kids ate the dill pickles, and every day they asked if she wanted more dill pickles and every day she got sick.

"Annie, what do you want me to buy?"

"Just underwear. That's all."

"Underwear? How do you buy underwear?"

"Easy. Anybody can buy underwear. That's the easiest thing to buy. All you have to say is: Size 48 Big."

"What?"

"Size 48 Big. Say it. Say 'Size 48 Big.' That's all. You want some licorice sticks, or don't you?"

"Oh, yes. Yes, I do."

"All right, then. Say 'Size 48 Big.'"

I had to tell her a hundred times before she finally got it.

"Now here's the money. What do you say?"

"Size 48 Big."

"Okay. Now go inside. I'll wait right here."

Again, she tripped. But she made it to the counter, hopping on one foot and looking back to see if I was still there.

"Size 48 Big," I mouthed, then stepped away from the door. So Sammy wouldn't see me.

Good ole Susie. I'll give her two pieces of candy. If Mr. Mandelblatt waits on her right away, I'll give her two pieces.

I waited . . . and I waited . . . and I waited. *What's keeping her?* I tip-toed to the window and peeked in. Mr. Mandelblatt was arguing with Mrs. Adams, Sammy was waiting on William Murray. But where was Susie?

Then I saw her, all scrooged up against the candy counter. *You dumb thing, Susie,* I thought. *Mr. Mandelblatt will NEVER see you there.*

I tried to get her attention. Instead, Mr. Mandelblatt saw me.

"Keep away from that window. You wanna buy something, come inside. Those kids," he continued yelling, "always dirtying up my windows."

Then he saw Susie. "Get away from that glass. You want candy, you come here."

That's when things began to happen. Susie came running out of the store.

"Annie, I forgot what."

"Size 48 Big." I blew the words into her face.

Again she came back. "Mr. Mandelblatt wants to know what."

"Un-der-wear, Susie. Un-der-wear," I mouthed.

Back inside I heard her shout, at the top of her voice, "UNDER-WEAR. ANNIE SAID UNDERWEAR."

Everything in the store stopped, every head turned. Mr. Mandelblatt began to move toward the door, Susie after him. I ran to the side of the store to hide, but Susie saw me.

"There she is. Annie, Annie. Come back, Annie."

I came.

Mr. Mandelblatt's face was all sweaty and splotchy red. Behind him was Susie, then Sammy.

"Oh, here she is, our fine lady. Vait vun minute, Annie, I bring everyt'ing out. Everyt'ing. So you can see for yourself."

"I--I was just s—standing here."

"Oh. You vas jus' standing. I see. Inside, also, are people jus' standing. Maybe you come inside and stand, eh? Come, come. Come into my store."

I followed.

Inside, there was underwear all over the counter.

"You vant backside mit buttons, or you vant mit snappers? *Over here Annie. The underwear is over here.* Or do you vant just flapped open?"

Now he was turning them over. "You vant mit double crotch, or — ANNIE, HERE. The underwear is HERE." As if I didn't know.

"Tell him, Annie. Tell him," nudged Susie. "Size 48 Big."

Mr. Mandelblatt was wiping his forehead. More people were coming into the store.

"Dese ole country pipple yet. Dey send dere children. I hafta be mind-READ-er. And if I giff just vun t'ing wrong, oi-yoi," he said, wiping his forehead again. "Annie, how much money your Mama giff?"

"Money? Susie, where's the money?"

She didn't have it. Not in one hand. Not in the other.

"Susie, what did you do with the money?"

She began to cry. Then I saw it: the handkerchief with the money down by the candy counter. I swooped it up and handed the whole thing to Mr. Mandelblatt and watched him untie the knot, muttering all the while, "dese ole country pipple."

After he had counted the money, he selected the underwear, wrapped it up and handed the package to me. "And tell your Mama nex' time come herself."

I couldn't get out of the store fast enough. "We hafta run, Susie."

"Run? But the candy. You didn't buy the candy."

"Candy? You think I'm crazy? I'll never buy anything in that store again."

"But you said."

"I don't care what I said. And if you won't come right now, I'll leave you here."

"But you didn't buy the candy." Susie was beginning to cry.

"And you didn't buy the underwear, so come." I had to pull her. "And don't cry. I'll buy some candy tomorrow. I'll buy it at Dickler's."

Flipping and flopping behind me, she began to run. Crying. By the time we got to our house, her face was so streaked I had to wipe it with her dress.

"Wanna come in? I'll give you a cookie."

"Okay."

"And quit sniffing. Mama will ask what's the matter."

Inside I gave the underwear to Mama, then picked up a cookie from a plate on the table. Mama had made a boxful for Uncle Fedor to take. "For Susie," I said.

I gave Susie a cookie and was about to ask her if she wanted to stay but decided against it. Instead I gave her another cookie.

"You can go home now, Susie."

"Okay."

Mary and Mikie were playing on the floor and the baby was sleeping. Mama was exulting over the underwear.

I was reaching for a cookie myself when I heard Mama. "Look," she was saying to Pap. "Maybe we send Annie to buy for you."

I couldn't believe what I heard.

I looked at Pap. He seemed to agree.

"I get the money," said Mama, disappearing into the back room.

I stood rooted to the floor, but only for a moment. Once in every lifetime comes an immediacy that would flip an orbiting planet into reverse. Mine had come. I jumped through the doorway and yelled, "COME BACK, SUSIE. COME BACK."

Mama at the Doctor's

I liked school but I was always glad to get home. As soon as I got into the kitchen, as soon as I called out "*Slava Isusu Christu,*" as soon as I saw Mama, then the kids, I was glad to be home.

But one day I stopped dead. Aunt Julie and Mrs. Murray were there, and Mama was sitting on a chair beside the stove, holding her stomach.

"What's wrong?" I asked.

"Women trouble," said Aunt Julie, as if I'm not supposed to know.

"Another baby?" I whispered.

"Keep quiet."

"I be all right," Mama was saying. "Diss happen before."

"All the more reason for you to go to a doctor," said Mrs. Murray.

"Ne-vair," Mama was saying. "I nevair go to man docktor. First I die."

"Then you'll die," said Mrs. Murray. "If you won't have a man doctor, you'll have a man undertaker."

Undertaker? "Mama, go. I'll go with you. I went with Mrs. Donelko and now she's all right."

"All the doctor will do," Mrs. Murray was saying, "is give you some pills. This happens to all ladies."

Finally, Mama decided to go. Aunt Julie helped her get dressed, then stayed to take care of the boarders and the kids.

When we got to the doctor's office, we found it full of people. No chairs. A man got up and gave Mama his seat. I smiled and said, "Thank you."

The man smiled back.

I watched him take a place against the wall. An Englishman, I could tell. Because he had manners. Englishmen always said "please" and "thank you" and "excuse me." And they gave their seats to ladies. Because their ancestors were Knights of the Round Table. I looked at him. Again he smiled at me.

"Mama," I whispered, "do we have ancestors?"

"What is that?" she said.

"The people who were here before all the grandfathers and all the grandmothers," I explained. Sometimes Mama was an exasperation. "What kind were they?"

"What kind? People. Like us," she said.

"Like us? What kind of ancestors is that?"

Mama said she didn't know. "I wasn't alive then."

Of course she wasn't alive. What a thing to say. I gave up and looked at the Englishman. He was reading a paper. Englishmen always read the paper, too.

"Next time," I whispered to Mama, "say 'thank you.'" But she wasn't listening. The pain.

I looked around at other people, those who came before us and those who came after us. To make Mama feel better I whispered, "Mostly ladies."

When we finally got into his office, the doctor looked at me and smiled.

"How old are you, Annie?" he asked. He remembered me from when I was there with Mrs. Donelko and from when I was there with Little Liza. Always he asked, "How old are you?" and always I said, "Almost ten years old."

To Mama he asked, "What seems to be the problem?"

"It's her s—stomach. When she e—eats she v— vomits. And she c—can't do any w—work. Aunt J—Julie c—comes."

"How many children?" asked the doctor.

I began to count. Sometimes I forgot the ones that died.

"S—six," I answered.

"How old is your mother?"

She answered, "*Dvacec oshem.*"

I translated, "Twenty-eight."

Mama could understand English. She just couldn't talk back. If we wanted something, like an apple, we spelled it out: a-p-p-l-e, so she wouldn't know.

Now the doctor was listening to her chest. Then he looked into her mouth.

"Say 'a-ah,'" he said.

"*Hutorce*, 'a-ah,'" I translated.

But Mama couldn't say "a-ah." She kept gagging.

"Don't gag," I said.

Aunt Julie said if Mama died, Pap would have to marry another lady and then I'd have a stepmother. Then I'd really have to work. "Mama, please say 'a-ah.'"

But she couldn't.

"Will she die?" I asked.

"No. She'll be all right. Don't you worry your little head about that. She'll be all right."

The doctor put away his things, asked Mama to get up, began feeling her stomach.

"Hurt?" he asked.

"Say 'yes,' Mama. Say it hurts."

The doctor then turned to me.

"I'll have to give her a better examination. Tell your mother to go behind that curtain. She'll have to slip off her undergarments."

"Undergarments?"

"So I can examine her."

He meant underwear. But how could I tell her?"

"Mama, he said, "y—you h—have t—take off your p—pants."

"*Co?*"

"The doctor said you h—have to—" I couldn't say that word again.

"Never. I die first."

"Shshssh. He'll hear you."

"I don't care if he hears me."

I peeked through the curtain. He was standing in the middle of the office, waiting, looking at his watch. Maybe if I stepped out.

"Mama, I'll wait for you outside."

"Don't go," she said.

"Mama— ."

"I won't. Tell the doctor I won't. Tell him I pay him and we go."

I stepped outside. "She w—won't," I said. "We'll p—pay you and we'll go."

"Annie, you go in there and tell your mother she's a very sick lady, and I'm going to examine her if I have to take off her — her — underwear myself."

I went back in. "That's what he said, Mama."

"I heard him."

"Okay. You stay. Just turn your head."

I did.

After the doctor had finished, he said, "You can turn around now, Annie."

Back in the office, the doctor asked Mama to sit down, then turned to me. "Annie, your mother will have to go to the hospital. To have her appendix removed."

"Hos-pi-tal?" Mama understood that word.

"No bad, no bad," the doctor said. He knew to talk our way. "Not to worry. No too bad."

On the way home, despite her pain, Mama cautioned me: "No say not'ing," but she didn't have to. As soon as Mama said, "*Na operaci- ju, do hospitalju,*" the wailing began.

"Call Mrs. Murray," Mama managed to say to me. When Mrs. Murray came, Mrs. Murray began to scold Mama.

"Don't be a baby."

That's all it took. The next day, Pap took off from work so he could take Mama to the hospital. But before they left, Mama called me into the bedroom.

"If I die, take care of Mary and Mikie," she said to me.

"I will, I will, Mama."

And all the day we prayed. Until Pap came home.

"The operation is over," he said. "Mama will be all right."

While Mama was in the hospital, Pap and I did the breakfasts, Aunt Julie and Aunt Liza took turns with the suppers, and in the eve- nings, because Pap had to go to the hospital — sometimes our Mary went with him — Uncle Mike and I did the dishes, and again, he teased: "You can get married now."

When the time came to bring Mama home, our Mary and I cleaned up, first the kitchen, then her bedroom. Aunt Julie had al- ready washed and hung the curtains, there was a new spread on the bed and new pillows. Soft. We fluffed the pillows, went over to the dresser, made sure everything was neat — made sure the Blessed Mother was turned so she could look at Mama.

And when Pap carried Mama into the bedroom and laid her gen- tly on the bed, I couldn't believe what I was seeing: As if he cared. I thought he was just Pap and Mama was just Mama, but he cared for her.

Donelkos' Pig

I was poking a stick into the water in the ditch making mud whorls. I had gotten the baby to sleep, Mary and Mikie were playing on the floor, and Uncle Mike was talking to Mama, so I thought to go outside and play. But I couldn't find anyone. Susie was probably minding their baby. That's why I was poking a stick into the water making mud whorls.

It had just finished raining and the water was running clear and clean, and if you stuck a stick away down in, then carefully pulled it out, a mud cloud would *froom* up, whirl around then swim down the ditch in a fast whirly tail. But if you pulled the stick out fast, you'd get a swoosh, and swooshes didn't go into tails.

I was trying to make one more tail when I heard a low *harruff* right behind me. I jumped. Then I knew: Donelkos' pig. She was rooting in the bushes where the Eyetalian kids threw their salami. Every day except Friday, their Eyetalian mothers gave them salami sandwiches, but the kids in school made fun of them, so they threw their salami into the bushes, and that's where Donelkos' pig was: rooting for salami. As fast as I could, I ran to tell Mrs. Donelko.

"Mrs. Donelko, Mrs. Donelko," I yelled. "Your pig, your pig," until she heard.

"Your pig," I cried again, pointing to the alley.

Shoving her kids back into the kitchen, she slammed the door shut, jumped down the steps and ran through the yard.

"Over there," I yelled, running after her. But the pig wasn't there. *Then I heard.* I had left our gate open and there she was: in with our chickens. The poor chickens were in one corner, all piled up on top of each other.

"Shoo, shoo!" I cried, then yelled for Mama, and when she saw, she ran back for a broom.

Mrs. Donelko already had Mama's clothes prop. Together they prodded and pushed. The clothes prop snapped. Mrs. Donelko picked up the sharpest point, Mama the other piece, but the pig wouldn't budge.

"Get me a rope," cried Mama to me.

But the rope kept sliding off into the mud. The pig fell. So did Mama. Quickly, Mrs. Donelko slid the rope around the pig's belly. The pig got up. Mama got up.

Together they pulled. But the pig pulled too, pulled the rope right out of Mrs. Donelko's hands, knocking her over.

"Hold it, hold it, Mama."

She did, with all her might. Mrs. Donelko grabbed her end, but when they got to the gate, there stood Susie, Mikey and Pauly — Susie still in her petticoat, Pauly in only a diaper, and Mikey with nothing on and he a boy!

"Go back," cried Mrs. Donelko.

"Stay with them," cried Mama to me.

I turned to Susie. "You stay. They're your kids."

The pig was heading for the dump, trailing the rope, down, down, toward the railroad tracks, we after her. Two brakemen were already waving their brakey clubs (clubs used to brake the speed of a car).

The pig didn't know which way to turn. She began to twirl on one hind leg, like a dancer, as if to fly, but how can a pig fly? Instead, she leaped past the brakemen, straight to the tracks, and stopped. Some wheat had fallen from some box cars, and no matter how hard the men pounded and clubbed, the pig would not budge. A freight train appeared and blew and blew its whistle, but the pig went on eating the wheat. The train had to stop. Out jumped the engineer and the fireman.

"Whose pig?" asked one of the men.

"Hers," I said, pointing to Mrs. Donelko, because that was the truth. And that's when we noticed our Mary and Mikey, then Susie, Mikey Donelko and Pauly. They had followed us down through the dump, Mikey Donelko still with no clothes on. Pauly, screaming, ran to his mother. Mrs. Donelko began to wail and wring her hands.

Mama cried to me, "Annie, go get a pan of middlin'. Run." I ran.

And that's all it took, some middlin' mix across the railroad yard, up the dump, up the alley, and into the pen.

Mama wrung the necks of the chickens that had been crushed. That evening we all had chicken soup — we had soup, and the Donelkos had soup.

WWI and the Mexicans

I must have read it somewhere, and it stuck: that one's every action, be it only a smile or a frown, goes on forever. Touching first the person exposed to the act, be it deliberate or accidental, it goes on, for better or worse, to touch the next person, then the next, and the next, until it not only encircles the globe, the act comes back again to the very person who initiated it in the first place. A kind of presentation, be it one of joy or one of despair, is going on all the time.

It was the rippling effect of a shot fired on the other side of the globe, in Sarejevo, that started World War I, that had me, a third grader, holding skeins of yarn between my two taut arms so that Mama could roll the yarn into balls, to knit sweaters. Mrs. Murray showed Mama how, Mama showed Aunt Julie and Aunt Liza and Mrs. Donelko, and every evening they came down to our house to knit for "our boys" overseas.

Every day a trainload of soldiers spilled out onto the Eastbound Hump, marched to the empty field across the tracks to exercise, then back on the train, and off to the War. "Over there," we sang.

> Over there, over there.
> Send the word, to beware, over there.
> That the Yanks are comin'.
> The Yanks are comin'.
> Their drums rum-tummin' everywhere.
>
> Over there, over there.
> Say a prayer to beware over there.
> We'll be over, we're comin' over.
> And we won't come back,
> 'Tis it's over, over there.

When all the boys were "over there," camps were built on the same field for Mexicans who came here to do the work on the railroad. There were three camp buildings: two for sleeping and one for the kitchen and dining room. The third building also housed the camp master and his wife.

The Mexicans weren't allowed over to our side of the Hump. The railroad bulls made sure of that, but I went over to their side. The camp master had a newspaper with funnies: "The Katzenjammer Kids," "Mandrake the Magician," "Hairbreadth Harry," and many others. Two full pages, and when I was finished, I folded the paper just the way it was. If I didn't, "You can't look at the paper anymore," said the camp lady.

Once Pap went over with me. He knew some of the Mexicans. They worked in the same gang with him, but all they did was smile at each other.

"They are good people," Pap said to Mama when we came home. "There is a cross over each door and a picture of the Blessed Mother on the wall — a Mexican praying before it. And before they eat a piece of bread, they make the sign of the cross. Just as we do."

But sometimes there was trouble; sometimes a fight. All the camp master had to do was pull a gun out from under the counter and lay it on top. I saw.

Most of the time, though, the Mexicans just talked and laughed, and if somebody played a guitar, they sang. And the songs they sang! First kind of sad, kind of lonely, then, all at once something happened, WOW, like wild.

Almost like a *czardas*. That's when the dancing started: first one man, then another and another, then everybody, like a snake dance — around and around, everybody clapping and yelling and stomping.

I danced, too, but the camp lady pulled me away. "Stay in the kitchen," she said. But that didn't stop my feet, and when I got home I showed Mary how, until Mama stopped us. "You're making the baby cry." But every chance I got, I ran over. Because of the funnies.

Sometimes a man would throw his hat on the floor. When he did that, everybody rose and danced around it. I tried that at home and again Mama hollered.

Another time a man pretended to be a lady. With a shirt tied around his waist, he wiggled his hips, this way and that, always somebody trying to pull the shirt off. Then he'd run, pretending embarrassment.

I was afraid of the camp master, because of the gun, but I liked his wife and she liked me. When mama made doughnuts, she sent some over for her. That's why she let me have the slop.

"You brreeng bokket," she said one day. "I geev you shlops. For peeg."

After thinking awhile, Pap said, "Give her two buckets. Small. Easier to carry." And that's when the trouble started.

When the Donelkos found out I was getting slop, they sent their Georgie over, but the camp lady gave it only to me. Even when Georgie began going over ahead of me, she still gave the slop only to me.

One evening I was waiting, both buckets full, for a train to go by and there was Georgie, hiding behind a cinder pile. I could see him.

Quickly, remembering the time he had upset my bucket of coal because the brakeman threw more coal in my direction, I grabbed both my buckets. This time I was determined not to let go.

"You get away from me, Georgie," I yelled, pretending not to be scared. "Don't you dare come near me."

But he did. He began pulling first one bucket then the other until I had to let one go. That's when he tripped and fell, the slop all over him, and there I stood, holding only one bucket.

"I didn't mean to do that," I cried, but he didn't care. He jumped up pulled the other bucket, dumped the slop all over me and ran.

"You're gonna get it now, Georgie," I cried after him. "Just you wait," but he was already across the tracks. I picked up the now-empty buckets and hurried before another freight train came.

When I got to our house, I was afraid to go inside. Slop all over me. *What would Mama say?* She heard me crying.

"What happened?" cried Mama.

And I told her. Everything.

Mama was washing my hair when Mrs. Donelko burst into the kitchen, screeching and yelling, pushing Georgie in front of her. When she saw Mama washing my hair, she stopped.

I peeked up at them. Georgie was hiding behind his mother, I could see. There was slop all the way down his pants and inside his shoe tops. He saw me peeking, stuck his hand into his pocket as if he didn't care, then pulled it right out again. There was slop in his pants pocket.

All at once, Mrs. Donelko began to laugh.

Mama began to laugh.

Soon we were all laughing. We couldn't stop.

Then Mrs. Donelko, still laughing, turned to leave, but first she pulled Georgie's hair, but not too hard, then she whacked him on his behind, but not too hard, so Mama wouldn't be mad at her.

And that was the last time I went over to the camps. Pap said, "Don't send her any more."

End of the War, End of an Era

One afternoon — we were almost home from school — we began to notice something different. ALL THE WHISTLES WERE BLOWING.

Normally, we paid no attention to them. The whistles were always blowing, always moving, but this was different. *The engines were standing still*, and so many, the sound coming from everywhere, louder and louder, from the Eastbound Hump, across the railroad yards, from the Westbound Hump, from the Engine House, from the Car Shops, all stopped in their places, blowing and blowing and blowing. And all the mothers were out of their houses.

"The end of the world," some were crying.

"Look. The men. They're all coming home from work."

"The end of the world."

But when the men grew closer, "END OF THE WAR," was the cry. "END OF THE WAR."

We, the kids, picked up the cry, "End of the War. End of the War."

By evening, after supper, after dishes, joy that the war was over was tinged with gloom.

"For us, the war is not over. Not until we hear something," Uncle Mike was saying. I knew what he meant. How many times I had heard him, when talking with Mama, say about his Mikie, "I wonder on which battlefield he is. Is he still alive?"

Uncle Fedor, too, had a son over there.

And they worried about the people. We had heard that whole villages had been destroyed; in one village, all the men had been slaughtered.

"No, for us the war is not over," repeated Uncle Mike.

"It is over for Mrs. Kelley," said Mama. Mrs. Kelley's son, Augustus, had been killed.

"And not for *Lipinska*." Her two sons were missing in action.

But the next day at school, the excitement returned. Flags were taken down for cleaning; some replaced. The firewagon was pulled out to be washed and painted. The Boys' Fife and Drum Corp. was reorganized. Everything was put into readiness for when the boys came marching home again.

At our house, we waited for the newspapers. *The Jednota* printed names of people still alive. Finally, a letter. I was barely inside the post office door when Emma Foerster cried, "Annie. A letter. Don't lose it."

And when I got home, Mama grabbed it and kissed it, then put it on the mantel for Gavaj to read when he got home.

The letter was for Big George, from his Tera.

"*Slava Isusu Christu*," the letter began properly. Again, properly, "I am in good health. I wish the same for you." Then, "Come home. Right away, come home." That was all.

Gavaj gave the letter to Big George, who at once began kissing it, every word.

When he came home from work the next day, he said, "Today I quit America. I go home."

Later we learned that Tera was pregnant, raped by soldiers going through the village. She and her sister had run into the loft to hide. They were found. Her sister had jumped out of a window, but Tera was not that lucky.

In a few days, a few more letters.

"How could one priest write so much?" Uncle Mike had said. One letter was for him.

Aunt Mary was in good health. So was little Susan. She had no news about their Mikie, but that was good. No news was good news. If he had been killed, she would have been notified.

There was so much destruction everywhere, Gavaj read. Some lost everything, but Aunt Mary was lucky.

Later it developed that because their hut was the best, it had been used as headquarters by the army, which is why the soldiers were good to her. She cooked for the officers and took care of the wounded.

Soldiers slept in all the huts; the people just moved over and slept anywhere. "Because they are fighting for our country," they said. When a soldier arrived wounded, the women took care of him. But there were atrocities.

"I will die before I live through another war," Aunt Mary had written.

The very next day, Uncle Fedor received a letter. Again, it began properly, "*Slava Isusu Christu*," then, "But I have no news of our Sandor."

"Maybe that is good," said Uncle Fedor, wiping his eyes.

Later we learned that when authorities had come through the village conscripting for the service, Aunt Mary hid Sandor in the chimney. When asked about him, she said she didn't know, but they didn't believe her. They thought he had run away to America.

For punishment, Aunt Mary was made to walk for weeks up and

down the village street with a heavy pack on her back until she couldn't walk any more. When Sandor finally came out of the chimney, he was almost blind. Because of the soot.

A letter came from Uncle George's wife.

"I expected that," said Pap. "What can we say?"

For over a year, maybe more, we hadn't heard from Uncle George. He had just quit coming. Pap looked everywhere: Braddock, Rankin, Duquesne, and nothing.

"I will try again," he said, and he did, and nothing.

Gavaj had to tell her.

Even though we didn't hear from Uncle George — he disappeared somewhere in America — Mama sent money.

More and more letters began to arrive. Grandma's letter said she was fine, she was lucky, she was spared because she was old. But not the others, and not the country. The mighty Austro-Hungarian Empire was no more. The money the people had sent – Pap, as did the others – all their savings for God and country because *Someday we go back*; *someday we live like "Grofs*", was no more. The dream went up in gun smoke.

Some of the men decided on staying another year to make up the money lost. Of every one that returned, two remained. Travel was now free between the two continents; our beds were filled quickly by another generation, children of those who came first. The dream was now The American Dream.

The first to come was Uncle Mike's son, Mishko, and son-in-law, Janos, to be greeted with, as were invariably all the others:

"Did you bring any new songs?"

"Wait until you hear!" was the ready response.

War songs they were: One about a father who had no sons to give to his country, but he did have three daughters. To each he sang, beginning with the eldest:

> You, I know, with one true mark.
> Would make another Joan of Arc.
>
> The first one cried, Not I, a soldier.
> The second 'murred, If I were older.
> When he asked his youngest daughter,
> Yes, she cried, I with not a falter.
> Dearest father, I will go.
> I will make our Country glow.
>
> When her uniform was tried,
> Her mother, and her father cried.

When her sword was girded on,
Her sisters fainted at her side.

And when she marched into the fray,
On her horse, without delay —
As church bells rang from dell to dell —
A hundred thousand Cossacks fell.

Another about a soldier saying good-bye to his beloved:

Will you wait for me, asked he,
Yes, oh yes, she cried, then he:
When the final battle's won,
I'll greet you like the morning sun.

And if by chance I come no more,
I'll wait for you at Heaven's door,
Where at last we'll be together,
Live in paradise forever.

While the Big Three, Clemenceau, Lloyd George and Woodrow Wilson, were drawing boundary lines, that to this day have yet to be made right, while money throughout all of Europe was not worth the "paper" it was printed on, hunger and distress becoming the lot of the masses, we in this country sang:

Amerika. Amerika.
Where money grows on trees.
Amerika. Amerika.
Where life is but a breeze.

If you come and live with me,
In silks and satins you will be.
Amerika. Amerika.
Where money grows on trees.

even though I heard Mama, one hot day, cry out, "If I am here one hundred years, one hundred babies I will have."

To which Pap ruefully replied, "Maybe the rich know something."

Still they came, their women after them. Always there was somebody new in our house, either from Europe or from another city looking for work, for a place to live. By the smell of their bags I could tell if they came by ship or by train.

The second wave of arrivals came not only with newer songs and newer stories, they came with a newer exuberance. They already knew what a dollar was. They stayed at our house just long enough to establish their own households.

Changes were also happening in our own family: Our family was getting bigger. Time had come to put away Old Country ways, time we lived like Americans. Time we had a parlor like the Murrays had. Time we took over the upstairs bedrooms. And Gavaj, the last of our boarders to go, saw it was time to go.

He found another boarding house, then another. None suited him. We expected that. He finally decided on living alone. But we missed him. When we met outside the church, we laughed to keep the tears from showing.

The transition from the old to the new was not simple at home either. There was the matter of naturalization, and no matter how hard he tried, Pap just couldn't say the words.

Mama could say the whole thing without even stopping to take a breath: "Aj plej-a-lii-djenc-tuu-da-flegg . . . ," (I pledge allegiance to the flag), but women didn't count. It was the father who had to go to the courthouse. When he became naturalized, his wife became a citizen automatically.

Finally, Pap made it. But it was Mama who was proud. Pap still missed the Old Country. Missed his mother.

And she missed him, too. Always, in her letters, she would say, "every day I wait."

Part III

Letter from Grandma

One day a letter came that changed all this. By then I could read Slovak, too, but we waited until everyone was home from work to read it.

"Praised be God," I read. "Praised be forever," was the answer. But I didn't read "I am well and wish the same for you." Instead I read:

"This letter is for Andrej Chizmar, beloved son of Suzanna Chizmar of the Village of Revisce, County of Ungvar." Then I read "Andrej, your mother is no more."

"No more," said Pap. "Read no more."

"Let us pray," said Uncle Mike. And we did.

"Our Father, Who art in Heaven, hallowed be Thy Name . . . " and when we came to *Vicnaja Pumnjat* — Eternal Memory — we could hardly sing for crying.

When we had finished, Pap rose. "To Julie's, to my sister," he said, then to me, "Go tell Aunt Liza."

As soon as Aunt Liza heard, she grabbed the baby. "Come," she said to Uncle Jakub.

Lizka and I joined hands and ran. When we got to our house, Aunt Julie and Uncle Maksim and Little Julie were already there, Aunt Julie already wailing.

"*Mamushka, mamushka*, you nursed me when I was a baby, when I fell you picked me up, you taught me right from wrong. *Mamushka, mamushka*," she wailed.

Then Aunt Liza, remembering something, began to wail. Then Mama. We all wailed.

When we were out of tears, Pap rose and left the kitchen.

"To the woodshed," said Uncle Mike.

Mama, already brewing a pot of tea, said, "Let him go."

After everybody had gone, after we were all in bed, it seemed that Grandma was still with us. I could feel it. All the while, I had been seeing her standing in the doorway of her hut, waiting for us to come, but now she was right here, with us. Her presence was everywhere. Always, in her letters, she would say, "Just once, if God would be so kind, let me hear your voices," and now it happened. She had come to us.

About Grandma

Grandma was as real to me as were Aunt Julie or Aunt Liza or anybody. Maybe more so. The image I had in my mind did not conflict with an actual presence. That is why, after the initial shock, the news of Grandma's death didn't change a thing. She was part of us before the letter came, so she was after the letter was read. We heard the words, but once they retreated, we began to feel her presence. She was, at last, with us.

And when Pap went to the woodshed, it was not to be alone — it was to be with Grandma. Sometimes I went down to join him. Sometimes we talked.

From bits and pieces stored in my memory, much like items found in a closet, I could assemble a picture of what it must have been like back there.

"How big was the hut?"

"Where did you sleep?"

Along one wall there were two cots, one for the very old and one for the very young. Others slept on the floor. Under each cot was a chest for linens.

In one corner was the stove, in another, a spinning wheel and a bench for shoe repairing. There was a door that led through a shed-like space to the outside, the *komora*. That's where food was stored, and that's where the chickens roosted.

"First one up let the chickens out."

Every hut had its own kitchen garden and fruit trees, and outside the *komora* door was an igloo-shaped earthen mound with an opening. This is where food from harvest to harvest was stored.

All the huts were in a row along one lane, a pattern established when people were still serfs, when all land was owned by a *Grof*. After land reform, the pattern remained. In America, it has been said, "If you can see the smoke of your neighbor's chimney, you're too close." Over there, all huts were close, the fields at a distance.

"A nice way to live," said Pap. "Neighbor helped neighbor. There was no hidden wealth, and when evening came, everybody went home together."

Every hut had an icon facing the East; the first thing anybody did upon entering was to bow toward the icon.

"Ours was of Saint Andrew," Pap once said. "The rich, like the

Grof's family, prayed to big saints like Saint Peter or Saint Paul, but for the poor, only a little saint would listen, and sometimes we weren't sure of that. Our Andrew must have been the poorest of all: no embroidery on his robe. Not like Saint George on the church wall: a spear in his hand and on a great white horse.

"All Andrew had was a crooked stick for a staff, plain old robes, and on his feet no sandals. On his day, if you wanted to, you could even clean out the stable. But he was ours. When Grandma gave him a lily at Easter time, then some greens at Pentecost, he looked real nice, and every evening after prayers I made him a promise: When I died I would take him up a pair of sandals, until one day I mentioned this to the postman and he laughed: 'Nobody wears shoes in Heaven. That's why only the poor go there.'

"The postman was right. The poor didn't have boots. Not until money began coming in from America did even the children begin to wear boots. Those who weren't so lucky eased their *ohorchenje* [chagrin] with taunts like, 'Ha, even their chickens wear shoes.'

"They had to make jokes somehow," Pap said. "Actually, when people began buying things above their station there was much disapproval. What will people say? When we began sending Grandma money, she begged us, 'Please for God's sake, don't put a floor in.'

Once, when talking about Grandma always wearing black, Pap said, "I can't imagine my mother was a young girl once with ribbons in her hair, that once she was a bride with a veil on her head, and that once she was a young matron proudly wearing an embroidered scarf."

"Why did the ladies all wear scarves?" I asked.

"A scarf was a mark of obedience to her husband, that she belonged to only him," Pap said. "And worn with pride.

"On her wedding day, at the end of the bridal dance, it was the wailful obligation of the mother to unpin the wedding veil:

> Just as once I left my mother,
> You must leave me for another.

After which it was the matron of honor's honor to pin up the bride's hair, over which she tied a scarf, to be worn forever, a symbol of now belonging to another, the mother wailing,

> No one ever will replace you.
> Let me once again embrace you.

"Mother and daughter had to be pried apart."

Neither could I imagine Grandma a young bride. More acceptable was a Grandma in black waiting for a letter. As if reading my thoughts, Pap once said, "Her life was not an easy one."

"What did you eat?"

"Potato soup and potato soup and potato soup. Sometimes with cabbage, sometimes with green beans, and sometimes just plain, with chunky pieces of black bread for dipping."

"Did you like it?"

"Like it? I have never yet sat down to a meal half as good, and if a piece of bread fell to the floor, we picked it up, kissed it, and ate it. On Sundays we sometimes had something different.

"Every Saturday, Grandma took care of Schruls' tavern. Saturday was the Schruls' Sabbath, and on the Sabbath a Jew did not touch money. Grandma collected it and placed it on the table. Sometimes she took me along. I got to play with their Itzik, and when Grandma was ready to leave, Itzik's mother gave us something. Once she gave us prune jam. That Sunday Grandma made *pirohi* [little pockets of dough]. Aunt Julie took some to the Schruls. The next time Mrs. Schrul gave Grandma extra.

"Grandma knew how to take care of sick people, too. When she was a little girl, she worked for a doctor; she knew about herbs and things — knew where to find them. And because she was a widow, she also helped in delivering babies. Somebody was always coming to our house. 'Come at once,' and Grandma went. Aunt Julie took care of us.

"One evening when Grandma was away," Pap told me once, "Aunt Julie and your Uncle George sneaked out during the night. When they returned, Aunt Julie's apron was full of peaches. Another time she brought apples. Until one night, they saw a *ghost*! They dropped everything and ran all the way home, the *ghost* after them, and never went out again.

"When Aunt Julie got big enough to work for a *Grof*, Grandma didn't stay away anymore, only to Schruls on Saturday.

"I looked forward to that; I got to play with Itzik and his mother always gave us something good to eat."

Peter

Pap, the youngest member of a "his children, her children, our children," family, was thirteen when he went to work for the *Grof*.

At thirteen, children were old enough to go out, the boys to stable work or to the miller's, the girls into homes as maids. By the time a girl reached fifteen, she was ready for marriage; at fifteen a boy was ready for America. That's when Uncle George left. Pap took his place at the *Grof's*.

Pap liked it there. The *Grof* had beautiful horses. Pap's job was to keep the stables clean and to help Krivda, the hostler.

And he had a good place to sleep: a nice corner all to himself, cool in the summertime and warm in the winter– time. He slept in the hay with Gazda the dog.

". . . I curled up in a straw tick with just my nose sticking out. When morning came, guess who pulled the tick off, then trotted beside me while I carried endless buckets of water for the horses? By the time Krivda arrived, we had already eaten."

"What did you eat?"

"Hot soup and black bread. Always hot soup and black bread."

"Did you like it?"

"What was there to like? When you're hungry you eat."

What we really wanted to hear about was Peter.

Peter was the *Grof's* only son, about the same age as Pap. Evenings, when the work was done and Krivda had gone for the day, Peter began coming down to sit with Pap.

Peter was a sickly boy, always having to swallow green medicines, always a nurse nearby. But when she brought Peter down to sit with Pap, she would leave them alone. Once Pap noticed that there was a young man at the back waiting to see her. But she never stayed too long.

Peter envied Pap's place in the hay. He liked the idea of Pap sleeping alone, nobody hovering over him. "I must sleep in a proper bed to grow properly tall," he would say, stretching his small body to the tallest, and eat everything on my plate to be properly healthy and properly strong," he would add, pushing his small stomach out to the fullest. Once Peter asked Pap, "Do you eat all your food?"

"All of it. More if I got it."

One evening, watching Pap eat, he asked, "Andruska, if I brought you some of my food, could I have some of your soup and bread?"

"Oh, yes," Pap agreed. When the exchange was made, Peter ate every bit of the soup and bread, but Peter's food? "No wonder Peter didn't like it." Said Pap. I didn't like it either," said Pap.

Looking back, Pap was certain that somebody in the big house was aware of this: that Peter's food went untouched. Peter began bringing fancy little cakes like marzipani. "A *kolachok* made in Heaven," Pap said, and always enough soup and black bread for both of them.

Still, Peter never stayed very long. After a short period, the nurse was back and Peter returned to the house, where, immediately, he appeared at the window to wave to Pap.

"He would wave, then I would wave, he would wave, then I would wave, until somebody pulled him away."

When cold weather came, Peter wasn't permitted out at all, so all they did was wave to each other. Sometimes, just to make Peter laugh, Pap played with the dog. Until one winter day...

It had been snowing all day, and as soon as Krivda left — he often left early to stop at the tavern — Pap ran out into the snow, the dog after him. With Peter watching from the window, Pap and dog rolled and coiled, the dog yapping and nipping until he became tired. Then Pap found a metal plate and began sliding down an embankment, falling off then jumping on, until soon the window was full of laughing faces.

The very next day, Peter's father came home with a sled. "Nothing in the world," said Pap, "could look even half as good as a brand-new sled, and in all the world there couldn't have been two more excited boys."

Peter began coming outside again, began to eat soup and bread again. He also began to put on weight and began to grow stronger. And, a little bolder.

One evening, Pap was beginning to think Peter wouldn't show up because of a big party at the house. But he kept his eyes on the house. Had the feeling that Peter would still come, and he did. He came from around the back, as if he were stealing away. And *no nurse*.

When almost at the stable, Peter leaped inside, stood before Pap, clicked his heels and saluted. With a grand flourish, he reached into his jacket and pulled out — *a bottle of wine*.

"Tonight," he cried, raising the bottle high, "we drink." That's all. He didn't know the next line. He looked at the bottle, but there was no help there, so he repeated, "Tonight, we drink."

Pap didn't know what to say either.

At a loss, Peter laid the bottle aside, sat down beside Pap, ate the soup Pap had saved, then picked up the bottle again.

"But we couldn't open it," said Pap. "We tried everything: our teeth, nails, a hammer, back to teeth, until finally, as if in anger, the cork popped out. Peter clamped his mouth over the gushing wine, I did the same, passed it back to Peter. When the fury in the bottle finally subsided, Peter wiped his mouth.

"'Good,' he said, handing the bottle to me.

"'Good,' I said, wiping my mouth, handing the bottle back to Peter.

"'The wine is very good.'

"'The wine is very good.'

"'The wine is very, very good.'

"'The wine is very, very good.'

"'Because we are friends,' said Peter, putting his arm around me.

"'Because we are friends,' I repeated, making a clumsy attempt at putting my arm around Peter. Failed. A poor boy wouldn't dare do that. But Peter expected it. I tried again. Fumbled and failed. In hysterics, we both fell into the hay."

The next thing Pap remembers is shrieks, a blinding sun, and more shrieks. The maids! Merka, screaming, was pointing at Pap, and Liska, screaming, was holding the empty wine bottle.

Peter, almost buried in the hay, was trying to get up. Merka jumped to help him up, Liska at the other side, all the while shaking her fist at Pap. "You'll get it for this."

Pulling and pushing, they managed to get Peter up. Slowly, Peter straightened his wobbly legs, then, just as they reached the doorway, Peter began to vomit.

"See what you did," they shrieked at Pap. "Just you wait. You'll get it for this."

After they had gone, Pap, feeling sick himself, rolled back into the hay. But he had to get up, and just as he reached the doorway, he, too, vomited.

By the time Krivda arrived, Pap had the place cleaned up, the water hauled. But the story got around and when Krivda heard it, he roared with laughter.

"Now," he said, putting an arm around Pap's shoulder, "now you are a man."

"But I didn't want to be a man," Pap told us. "Peter wasn't allowed out anymore and I missed him. He missed me, too. Sometimes, from his window, he'd wave to me and I'd wave back. That was all."

One day, lying in the hay, Pap began to hear the sound of a flute.

He knew it was a flute because Itzik's brother used to play one. Somebody was learning how to play the flute and he wondered if it were Peter. It was. "When the notes developed into a melody, Peter came to the window, waved to me and played for me. I clapped my hands, so happy to be part of his life again.

"Every evening, Peter played and I clapped, until, miracle of miracles, Peter was permitted to come out again. With his flute. First we ate [Pap thought that was the real reason Peter was permitted out: so he would eat], then the flute. Peter let me play, until it got so that I was playing more than Peter. Peter was becoming a little tired of the flute.

"Once, Peter's father came down to listen, but it was I who did most of the playing. When his father walked away I felt a little sad. But the very next day he brought another flute. For me. Before long, Peter and I played together.

"One day, Peter's mother came to listen. She was so delighted she arranged for a gathering of friends just to hear us.

"I was given a bath, which I hated, dressed in a velvet suit, which I liked, and patent leather shoes that hurt. I played, first with Peter, then alone, and everybody clapped.

"Afterwards, I was invited to eat with them but I couldn't eat. Everything looked good, but I never saw that kind of food — couldn't eat it. Peter didn't eat either. When Peter asked, 'Could we go now?' I was glad.

"After we changed, Peter's mother wrapped some food in a *khlebovka* and when we got to my place, we jumped into the hay and wolfed down the food in one gulp."

Pap and Peter continued to play the flutes, "but more and more, Peter was getting tireder and tireder. Sometimes he didn't come out at all, but we still played the flutes together, he from his window and I from the yard."

Pap stayed at the *Grof's* until he was sixteen. By then, Peter didn't come out at all.

That was when Uncle George returned from America. Time had come for him to marry.

With American money in every pocket, it wasn't hard for the *ohlednici* to find a bride for Uncle George: Aunt Ersa. In three weeks' time, the dress was made, the veil fashioned, chickens fattened, baking done, dishes borrowed, and last but not least, a horse and carriage regally decorated.

Also, downplayed by the wedding, something else was happening. Pap was preparing to leave for America.

But alas, life has a way of pouncing down on the brightest of occasions. In the midst of all the excitement, Peter died.

After the wedding, after the funeral, Pap's plans to leave for America were made final. On his last day, the *Grof* himself came to say good-bye.

"May God's angels watch over you," he said to Pap, then, reaching into an inside pocket, he brought out Peter's flute.

"From Peter," he said.

In America, the flute found its own niche: Pap's private place in the woodshed. That is where we sometimes heard him.

"Talking to Peter," Uncle Fedor would say.

And that is where Pap went, after Grandma's letter was read. After everyone had cried, after everyone had prayed, after Aunt Julie and Aunt Liza and the rest had gone home, after we were all in our bed, I could hear the flute.

All American's Day

After Grandma's letter, Pap became resigned to staying in this country. We were already somewhat acclimated, somewhat assimilated, but the old to the new had its frustrations. Many never could adjust.

Our food wasn't like "theirs," our mothers didn't dress like "their" mothers dressed. We didn't talk the way "they" did. We had an *accent*.

And our names. The girls were all either Annie, Mary, Lizzie or Suzie; the boys: Johnny, Mikie, Stevie, Pauly. As for our last names? If we could, we would have obliterated them. Full of meaning in their own right, the English tongue rendered them unpronounceable and ridiculous. Many were Anglicized. Some changed completely.

But at school, I must say, the teachers, on the whole, were very understanding. Especially Miss Mellon. It was she who said to Mama one day at the post office, "Don't let Annie wear that long black underwear. It shows when she tries to jump rope," and Mama complied. The black underwear disappeared. One thing about Mama: She was very quick on picking up the new ways. And Miss Mellon understood.

That was probably why, when the School Board asked for a child of the foreign class to recite "The Gettysburg Address" on All Americans Day, they asked Miss Mellon. And that is why, one day, the four of us were on our way to Miss Mellon's office: Rose Fontinello, Bernie Rubin, Sillian Silianoff, and me, where, after congratulating each one of us — after saying that only one of us will be chosen — she gave us over to Miss Irvine.

"You will each recite the same two poems," said Miss Irvine, "'Little Boy Blue' and 'The Wreck of the Hesperus,'" and I knew them both. And I loved to recite. When I recited I didn't stammer. In class when I recited "Little Boy Blue," Ella Marie had tears in her eyes.

And this time again, when it was my turn to recite, when I recited "Little Boy Blue," Miss Mellon smiled. And when I began "The Wreck of the Hesperus," at once I was out there on the ocean.

A fisherman stood aghast,
　　To see the form of a maiden fair,
　　Lashed close to a drifting mast,

and when I finished with:

　　Save us all from a death like this,
　　On the reef of Norman's woe,

they were all looking at me. Because I didn't stammer. Not even once.

The very next day, Miss Irvine told me, "Miss Mellon gave the part to you. But you'll have to work hard. You'll have to stay in every evening after school."

"Oh, I w—will, I w—will, M—Miss Irvine. I'll s—stay e—every e—evening. I'll ask my m—mother."

Not until I was outside and on my way home did I realize what had happened. All the way I ran, to tell Mama, to tell Pap. But mostly to be the first to get Pap's lunch bucket. Pap always saved his fruit for us, and the first there got it, but when I got to the gate, Mary and Mikey were already there.

"Pa-ap."

"An-nie," he mocked, handing the bucket to me, but Mikey already had the orange. "How many time I tell you: already no run. You big now."

"I k—know, but PAP . . . ." I began to yell. "TODAY I WAS PICKED . . . ."

"Now who pick on you?"

"N—no, P—Pap. It was MISS MELLON."

But already there was so much racket nobody could hear anybody. Mary was taking the orange from Mikie, Mikie, squealing, was not about to let it go. Mama, at the door with the baby, began scolding Pap, "You always do this: frightening the baby."

Now the baby was making more noise than anybody; all but Georgie. He was just standing there. So I grabbed the orange from Mikie and gave it to Georgie and that made it worse: Mikie began to squeal.

"Give me that orange," yelled Mama, handing me the baby. Now Georgie was crying.

But as soon as Mama began to separate the orange parts and everybody got a piece, all was quiet. *Now*, I thought.

"Mama," I began, "today I was p—picked to—to say the s—speech. The GET-TYS-BURG AD-DRESS."

"A dress? Whose dress?"

"N—not a d—dress, M—Mama. And GETTYSBURG is not a WHO. GETTYSBURG is a PLACE. L—like BRADDOCK. Th—there was a w—war, Mama. You know what a war is? It's where p—people fight and get k-killed, and . . . ."

But Mama wasn't listening. Mary was trying to exchange her piece of orange with Georgie because his was bigger, but he was already shoving it into his mouth and Mama was busy squeezing juice into the baby's mouth, so I turned to Pap.

". . . with m—men in gray, and m—men in blue, Pap, ALL SHOT UP and BLOOD ALL OVER," shouting toward Mama so she could hear too, and she did.

"There'll be blood all over this house if this keeps up." What did mama know?

I turned to Pap again. "When a—all the s—soldiers were killed, L—Lincoln c—came and m—made a s—speech, 'Fourscore and seven years ago.' Lincoln was the PRES-I-dent."

"President, eh?" Pap nodded his head and smiled. He always smiled when I used big English words.

"Yes, Pap, and I'm g—going to s—say the s—speech."

It was hard for me to talk with all the kids talking, but when Aunt Julie came down, Mama asked me to tell her. All she said was "Hmmmmmmff."

But when Mrs. Murray came over, she knew. She'd already heard. That's why she came over. She was as excited as I was. "That is a great honor," she said. "To speak on All Americans Day is a great honor. A big thing."

"Big?"

"See, Mama?"

"Yes," continued Mrs. Murray. "All the people will be there."

Mama didn't know what to say. "Like I make Annie new dress, maybe?"

A new dress? I looked at Pap. Pap thought Mama extravagant, but he wasn't saying anything. Neither was Mama. But Mrs. Murray was.

"No," she said. "Don't *make* her a dress. *Buy* her a dress. And shoes. Because everybody will be there. Everybody will be looking at her."

A *bought* dress. And *shoes.* Quickly my mind raced to the pink organdy in Mandelblatt's window, then to the shoes, black patent leather with rows of buttons. I could have hugged Mrs. Murray. If ever she wanted me to go to the store for her, I'd go. I'd go anywhere for her; help Bridget take the laundry to Mrs. Petrosky's. Anything. Now she was saying something else.

"Mrs. Murray, what did you say?"

"I'll make you curls. The night before I'll come over and put your hair up in rags. You'll have beautiful curls. You have beautiful hair."

I touched my hair. "I do?"

Pap was smiling, too. This time I wouldn't disappoint him, not like the time he introduced me to his boss.

"Why didn't you talk?" Mama asked me later. But I couldn't say a word; I was too scared.

Oh, I knew Pap was disappointed. But not this time.

The following days were unbelievable: Mama bought the dress and the shoes and Mr. Mandelblatt was as excited as I was. He threw in the petticoat and socks for nothing. "We're all going to be proud of you," he said.

Then came weeks of practice, every evening after school, and again at home. "Say, 'Forr-skorr" Mama would ask and I would rise, make a deep curtsy and begin, "Fourscore and seven years ago . . . ." without one stammer.

But in school it wasn't that easy. "Annie," Miss Irvine kept saying, "you're sing-songing again. Think of the dead. Think of the wounded. Think of their families, the blood that was shed, red, all over . . . ."

But all I could see was pink. Pink organdy.

One tired evening Miss Irvine said, "Annie, this will be the last try. If you can't do better we'll have to give the part to someone else. This morning I talked with Miss Mellon and she said . . . ."

"Oh, no. I'll do it. I'll do it. I know I can." But the only way I could see dead people was lying in a silk casket with beautiful carnations all around, all dressed up, ready for Heaven, to forever live with angels.

"Torn and mangled," Miss Irvine was saying. "You must see that."

Then I remembered. The bird. It had fallen out of its nest, and if I had hurried I would have picked it up, but the cat got it first so I grabbed the cat. But the cat wouldn't let go. Just wouldn't let go. And the mama bird was screeching something awful and I was screaming, "Pap, Pap," and he came running, but he was too late. The bird was lying on the ground, wings all torn and mangled.

"Torn and mangled," Miss Irvine was saying.

After that, when I came to the part about the battlefield I thought of the bird, about its wings. Miss Irvine began to nod her head.

Came the day. "Annie, you have to eat," said Mama. "You'll faint up there."

Faint! I couldn't faint if I tried. I couldn't even stand still so how could I faint?" But just to please Mama, I drank a little tea.

When Mrs. Murray came down to do my hair, I was already dressed. The night before, she had put my hair up in rags; now she came over to take the rags out. And everybody watched. Pap, too, and Uncle Mike. They had never seen anything like this before. Nobody had.

Standing me in front of her, Mrs. Murray began, and each time she untied a rag, a curl fell out.

"Beautiful," she kept saying.

"Beautiful," nodded Mama.

A curl fell over my shoulder. I touched it, then held my breath, as if only by holding my breath could I keep it real.

Then came time to leave. Pap held the door for me to pass through and the way he looked at me — different than at other times — not at my dress, not at my hair, but at me, deep into the inside of me. Quickly, from deep inside of me, I kissed him.

"Bye, Pap." This time I would not disappoint him.

When I stepped onto the porch, the Murray girls were already waiting.

We walked, one on either side, I in the middle, until we came to Mahans, when Elsie took Margaret's place, and when we got to McDonald's, Bridget stepped back to Eleanor. By the time we got to the schoolhouse, I was walking with Elizabeth Stansfield and Mary Etta Croft.

And when we walked into the classroom, everybody turned in their seats. Nothing could match that moment, and nothing could deflate it — not even Miss Irvine's caustic comment: "Well, we were beginning to wonder whether or not you'd even come today."

Wouldn't even come! Quickly I made my way to my seat.

Things were already beginning to happen. As soon as we pledged allegiance to the flag, the boys were excused to help outside with the chairs. The rest of us were permitted to stand at the windows and watch, and we did. Again, Elizabeth and Mary Etta stood on either side of me.

So many people. Elizabeth saw her mother and father and waved to them. Her mother was dressed in a dark blue suit and white blouse, a hat with daisies all around, and gloves. White. When she waved her hand you could see. She didn't even look like a mother.

Mary Etta saw her father talking with some men. "The school board," she said. And more and more people. "Isn't this exciting?" she cried.

Then Elizabeth, "Looky, looky, that funny man," she cried, pointing in the direction of the seats.

And I repeating, "That funny man." Then I saw: *It was Pap.* People were making room for him *in the front row*. Pap, in a tight jacket he saves for good, no necktie, shoes with double soles, not wanting to sit down but someone was making him, holding his cap with both hands. *Why did he hafta come?* I could have told him.

"I wonder who he is?" continued Elizabeth.

"Yes, I wonder," laughed Mary Etta.

And I, suddenly alone in a strange, strange world, looked straight ahead, and repeated, "I wonder who."

The next few minutes were a void, filled with separate and senseless sounds: Miss Irvine herding the class into line, Miss Irvine cautioning all to behave in their seats, Miss Irvine and I walking together toward the platform, where I was introduced to the members of the school board, then shown to my seat.

"You'll sit here until your name is called," Miss Irvine said, then left for a seat in the front row. I watched her until she was seated, then looked sideways to where Pap was. I could see his big, double-soled shoes. All the other men wore half-shoes with thin soles, but his were double.

And his hands: big, rough and red, holding his cap. The other men wore hats, but Pap? — he had to wear a cap.

Now the band was beginning to play "The Star Spangled Banner" and everybody was getting up. All but him. *Stand up, Pap.* He did. And everybody sang — everybody but him. All he did was twist his cap and look at me. *Why did he have to look at me? Why did he have to come? That funny man.*

Mary Etta's father gave a speech about national origins, about immigrants, and everybody clapped, and then it was my turn. "You're next," he whispered to me.

"And now," he was saying in a loud voice, "we will hear from the daughter of one of the newcomers to this country. Ladies and gentlemen, it is my pleasure to introduce to you, Annie Chizmar," and everybody clapped. Miss Irvine was motioning for me to rise and I did. Then she motioned for me to come forward, and I did. The clapping began to die down. Then only a few claps. Then there was only me.

I wanted to die, but not with Pap sitting there. I looked at Miss Irvine. She was mouthing the words, "Fourscore and seven years. . . ." I started, keeping my eyes on her, and as she mouthed the words, nodding her head, I continued, exactly as we had rehearsed, but when we came to "met on a great battlefield," I stopped. In terror, I looked at Pap. He seemed to want to jump out of his seat to come up and get me. His hands were praying — opening and praying. I saw the bird, in his hands, and my voice came back. "WE ARE MET ON A GREAT BATTLEFIELD OF THAT WAR . . . ." and as soon as I am finished, my thoughts raced, *I'll go down there beside my father and tell the whole world, "This is my father"* — Elizabeth and Mary Etta and everybody.

My voice had never been so clear and strong, and when I finished with, "THAT THIS GOVERNMENT SHALL NOT PERISH FROM THE EARTH," everybody clapped. They rose from their seats and clapped.

Miss Irvine ran up to the platform and couldn't stop hugging me. Mary Etta's father shook my hand again and again. And the people, all of them saying, "Annie, you were wonderful!"

I looked to see if Pap was still there, and he was. All by himself, squeezing and twisting his cap, looking at me, and I — I looked away. "That funny man," they had cried.

The next time I looked, he wasn't there.

Elizabeth held onto me, jumping up and down. "Mama wants you to come to our house for dinner. Could you, Annie? Could you?" And I said I could, but I had to let Mama know. Susie. I had just seen her standing near the platform, looking at me, and there she was, still looking. "Susie, will you tell Mama I won't be coming home? I'm going to Elizabeth's house."

"Okay, Annie. I will." She made a few steps toward me then stopped. Elizabeth was already pulling me by the hand, as if I were her very best friend. *Go away, Susie*, I thought.

At Elizabeth's, we went straight to her bedroom, her very own, with ruffles and curtains and dolls: a doll on her bed and a doll in every chair.

Once I had a doll. Once a man came to our house, greeted everybody, and when he noticed me sitting near the stove, he came right over and *handed me a doll. Me?* He didn't know I was the oldest, but I took it.

The doll had on a pretty pink dress, white shoes with pink socks, and a pink ribbon in her hair, and when I laid her down, she closed her eyes, and when I picked her up again, she opened them. *Play fast, play fast*, I thought, *before Mary comes in*. And I did.

Quickly, so as not to lose any time, I jumped off the chair, ran into Mama's bedroom, laid the doll on Mama's bed, watched as she closed her eyes, covered her up, then into the kitchen, onto the chair, swung my legs, off the chair, into the bedroom, picked up the doll, watched as she opened her eyes, carried her into the kitchen, held her in my lap, back into the bedroom, back and forth, back and forth, until Mary came in, and as soon as she saw the doll, it wasn't mine anymore.

Before the evening was over, the doll was broken: one leg off, her head askew, lying in the corner. Mary didn't want it any more. But forever, in my memory, once I had a doll.

But Elizabeth didn't have a little sister. Every doll in the house was hers.

Then I began to wonder: *What was Mary doing? What was everybody doing?*

We were playing "Uncle Wiggley" when Elizabeth's mother called for us to come down. "Dinner's ready," she called.

"Dinner," she said. Not "supper." *I'll have to tell Mama.*

"Come," said Elizabeth.

Downstairs, we went straight to the dining room. The Stansfields had a dining room with a chandelier and china closet. The table was set with beautiful blue plates and saucers, all the same kind, none chipped, and napkins. Blue. *Wait 'til I tell Mama.*

"Sit here beside Elizabeth," said Elizabeth's mother. I did.

Mr. Stansfield was already at the table – his coat still on. *Maybe he had another meeting. Maybe he had to hurry.* I hoped so. He scared me. But he didn't seem in a hurry. Maybe that is how he ate: with his coat on.

Mrs. Stansfield was putting the food on the table, smiling at me. I smiled back. But nobody was reaching for anything. Not until she sat down. And not even then. First Mr. Stansfield said grace, and not then either. Instead, everybody reached for a napkin and spread it across their knees. I did, too.

That's when Mr. Stansfield picked up first one bowl, then another, and another. That is the way they ate, everybody taking a tiny bit, and everybody saying, "Thank you."

"Have some, Annie," said Mrs. Stansfield, and I did. But I couldn't eat the way they ate — teeny little bites.

Besides, I didn't know what it was. I began to wonder what it was they were having at home. Maybe *halushki*. Maybe Mama will save me some.

"Elizabeth, I have to go," I whispered, sliding out of my chair, half of me measuring the distance to the door. Elizabeth was already out of her chair, Mrs. Stansfield was getting up. "I have to go," I heard myself saying.

"That's all right, Annie." Mr. Stansfield came over and patted me on the head. "We understand. Come over any time."

"Okay."

When Elizabeth opened the door, I discovered to my dismay that night had fallen. Without saying good-bye, I leaped off their porch and began to run.

Not until I got to our gate did I stop, then tip-toed through the yard and up to the porch. The kitchen lights were on so I could see inside: everybody there just sitting around and talking. Dishes all washed. I didn't know what to do. I began to retreat, wishing it were still last night — last night, taking one more peek at my dress, trying it on. I remember feeling so good I wanted to dance, but couldn't.

Not upstairs. So I stole downstairs, then softly out of the front door, where I twirled and danced as if forever. When I came to the edge of the porch, I stopped and curtsied, pretending I had already said the speech, pretending the whole world had listened — that the very stars had stopped to listen. Again I twirled, then curtsied to the stars. "Sorry, dear star, but I must go now. Because tomorrow . . . tomorrow . . . ."

Now it *was* — tomorrow. Now it was all over.

I peeked in the window. Everybody. Aunt Julie, Uncle Mike, the kids, everybody. Pap, back at the stove, fussing with some kindling wood. I wished I were dead. *If they found me dead, on the porch, in my new pink dress, would they be sorry?* I could just see it all: finding me. First Mama, then Pap, then the rest, straining to see. Then crying. Even Aunt Julie. Pap looking at me, all crumpled up in my pink dress, very sadly picking me up, curls trailing almost to the floor. Then I sneezed. I heard the door open. I tried to hide. But it was too late.

"Annie, it's you?" That was Mama. The kids exploded, jumping up and down, up and down. "Our Annie's home, our Annie's home." Pap was still at the stove, fussing with the kindling wood.

Now I was in the middle of the room, Mama turning me around and around, this way and that. "Who vas dere, Annie?" she asked, standing off, the better to see me. "What vas dere? Your Papa, he say not'ing. He vas dere and he say not'ing. Vas Fad'er Sandor dere?"

"Yes, Mama."

"Did he see you?"

"Yes, Mama."

"Did he say somet'ing? Vat did he say?"

"He said . . . he said . . . " Pap was matching two sticks of wood together.

"Vat did Fad'er Sandor say, Annie?" Mama continued, twirling me around again.

"He said, 'Annie, we are p-proud of you.'"

"He said dat? Fad'er Sandor? Papa, you hear? Fad'er Sandor said 'Ve proud.' Vas Mrs. Murray? Vas Mrs. Simmons?"

"Yes, Mama."

"Did they see you?"

"Yes, Mama."

"Vat did they say?"

"They said they were — p—proud — of me."

"Papa, you hear? They say they were proud."

Pap wasn't saying anything — not even looking at me. Just busy with that kindling wood.

But when Aunt Julie said, "Vell, I guess now you t'ink you are somebody?" he said, still not looking at me, "She is somebody. If you had seen her — if you had seen her today, if you had heard her, if you had heard all the people clap, you, too, would have been proud."

"Vel-l-l," Aunt Julie started, then stopped. That's when Mama clapped her hands. She could tell when something wasn't altogether right.

"Enough, already. Annie, upstairs. Change your dress. Time to put the little ones to sleep."

I went up, took off my dress and laid it, tenderly, between tissues, into its box. *Like into a coffin*, I thought. Then I went downstairs to wash the kids.

After prayers — Pap prayed with us — we went upstairs, and nothing. Pap said nothing to me. And I wondered, *would he come up, as he always did, before I fell asleep?* If he didn't, I'd die. But he did. He came in and touched my head. "Good-night, *Hanicka*," he said, and I replied, "Good-night, Pap," and it was worse than if he hadn't come in at all.

In the morning I waited until Pap left for work before going downstairs. Mama was clearing the table, but when she saw me she stopped.

"You still have the curls," she said. "If I comb your hair very carefully. . . ."

"No, Mama. Just braid my hair."

"Braid your hair?"

"Yes, Mama."

Off School One Day

But when I got to school, after All Americans Day, I began to wish I had let Mama comb my hair back into curls; everybody ran to me, remembering "Annie, Annie."

Elizabeth, too. "Mama said to come again."

"I will, I will."

But, alas, after a few days my fame began to trickle away. The girls went back into their own circles. Soon I was just plain Annie again. I would have done anything to be one of them. Maybe that was the reason I didn't go to school one day. Besides, if Elizabeth Stansfield and Ella Marie hadn't been off school that day to buy things, it would never have occurred to Elsie Simmons and me to play hooky. But they were off, and when they came back I could hardly believe all the things their mothers bought: dresses, two for each, scarves with jeweled clips, petticoats with ruffles and lace, and shoes with straps and pearl buttons.

That evening I was swinging the baby to sleep and trying to tell Susie Donelko all about it, but all she did was push her hair away from her eyes and look at me. There was no use in talking to her. She probably never heard of a store-bought dress. Once Mama gave her one of my dresses and she thought it was the grandest thing: preened around in it, ran home to show her mother then right back to sit on a chair, as if the dress were made of silk or something, smoothing it down and touching it like it was made of velvet.

"Susie, you don't know very much."

"Yes, I do, Annie. I know something."

"What do you know?"

"I don't know. Something."

That's when I noticed Elsie Simmons coming out onto her porch. The Simmons were English. We didn't go to their house and they didn't come to ours. They didn't go to the Murrays either, because the Murrays were Irish, but sometimes Elsie and I would talk. We were in the same grade.

"Wanna come down?" I called to her.

"Okay."

"You can go home now, Susie." She didn't budge. "Go, Susie." She went.

As soon as Elsie hopped up on the porch, as soon as she sat down, we began about Elizabeth and Ella Marie.

"They must be rich."

"Yeah. Maybe their fathers are brakemen."

"Or firemen. Or engineers. My mama said engineers make more money than anybody."

"They get to sit by the window."

"Yeah."

That's when the idea hit me. "Elsie, let's pretend our fathers are engineers. We could buy anything we wanted to. Take days off from school just to buy things."

"Yeah. Anytime we wanted to."

"Then, the next day, tell all the kids."

"Yeah."

"If we didn't go to school one day — just one day — we would tell the kids our mothers took us shopping."

"Could we? When?"

"Anytime. Tomorrow if we wanted to." It wasn't often Elsie came down to sit with me, nobody else around, just the two of us, and one whole day with just Elsie was more than I could believe. "Tomorrow, if we wanted to," I repeated. "Okay?"

"Okay."

"We can get up in the morning, walk real slow, then when all the kids are gone, turn around and not go to school at all. Then the next day . . . ."

"Can I go too, Annie? Can I?" It was Susie's voice.

"Susie, I thought you went home."

Susie began to sidle up to the porch.

"What'll we do?" said Elsie. "She heard."

Susie, her arms around the porch post, was swinging, first one leg then the other.

"She'll tell," whispered Elsie.

"Susie, will you tell?"

"No, I won't." She stiffened like a soldier boy, straight up and down. "Crisscross my heart and hope to die," she said, crossing herself almost down to her toes.

"Maybe we better take her along," I said.

"So she won't tell."

"If you tell, Susie, you'll get a beatin'."

"I won't, I won't. Crisscross . . . ."

"That's all right, Susie. We believe you."

She still made a cross, from the top of her head to the tips of her toes, like at the Veneration. I could see Elsie beginning to laugh. English people didn't do that.

"Stop it, Susie."

The next morning, Susie, lunchbox in hand, was already at the gate. As soon as Elsie came around the back, we huddled together, waiting for the kids to be gone. All but Joseph O'Hara, but he was always late, and when he saw us standing there he must have thought he had plenty of time. He began poking along, looking back at us.

"You'd better run, Joseph," said Elsie in a loud whisper. "You'll be late. 'Cause we're not going to school."

" 'Cause we're going shopping," I added.

We giggled to see him run. After he had gone, there was nobody. Just we three. "What shall we do?"

"I don't know."

"Let's go down to the railroad tracks."

We flew across the road before somebody could see us, then stealthily passed Mr. Adamson's shanty so he wouldn't see us.

"Don't let him see you, Susie," I cautioned.

"I won't."

Mr. Adamson lived alone in one of the shanties near the railroad tracks. We called him "that dirty old man." Once we got close enough to peek in and he saw us — came out smiling with his dirty old mouth, so we ran.

Once past Mr. Adamson's shanty we began to run again, down the path, down, down until we came to the cinder path.

"How quiet."

"Yeah. Nobody around. Just us."

"What shall we do?"

"I don't know."

We watched Susie, already jumping hopscotch. No lines. Nothing. Just hopscotching up and down and around.

"Susie, you have to have lines." I picked up a stone and made some lines. "There."

Soon, all three of us were hopping, crisscrossing, turning, then hopping again, Susie still stepping on the lines.

"Don't step on the lines, Susie. No wonder you're always out." But no matter how much I hollered at her, there she was, out again. So she quit. She went over to the rails and began walking on one rail, in one straight line, her arms out like a bird, and that looked like more fun than hopscotching.

> Rail-away and rail-around.
> Hop and hop and don't fall down.
> Don't fall down because you'll drown.
> Hop once more then turn around.

We hopped until we heard the sound of an engine: first the whistle, then a big engine with smoke as high as the sky, coming around the bend, then the freight cars.

When the engine came by, we waved to the engineer. He waved back then shook a finger at us.

We waved again to him, shook a finger at him, then stood, straight and still, as the freight cars went by. If you stood straight and still and didn't take your eyes off the cars, it's as if you were moving and the cars were standing still. We began to sing out the names:

"CHICAGO, MILWAUKEE AND ST. PAUL,"
"NEW YORK, NEW HAVEN AND HARTFORD,"
"THE BURLINGTON AND THE MISSOURI,"
"DENVER AND THE RIO GRANDE,"
and "THE PENNSYLVANIA."

Places full of wonder.

We stood that way until the caboose came along. Then you couldn't pretend any more. We had been all over the world and hadn't moved a bit. The man in the caboose waved a finger at us, we waved our fingers at him. Now that we had started, naughtiness was beginning to take hold.

"Elsie, let's pretend we really went some place."

"Where?"

"Any place. Far away. Where people have bazaars. Where people sell things on streets."

"Okay."

"Over here." I turned to a row of bushes on the other side of the cinder path. "Over here are the counters. And over there" — I pointed to the trees that were bending their branches toward the bush clumps — "over there are the clerks. Okay?

"Let me see," I went on. "I think I'll buy this pink chiffon dress. See? Easy."

"And I'll have this blue chiffon," said Elsie.

"And I — let me see — this blouse for Mama."

On and on we went, getting more extravagant by the minute.

For the most part, Susie just pranced and twirled and hopped, but she kept her ears open. Looking at her I said, "Imagine Susie in a gown with a long train."

"Yeah. And gold braid and ermine."

"One twirl and she'd fall flat on her face."

"Her feet waving in the air."

We couldn't stop laughing, and Susie, not knowing at first we were laughing at her, laughed, too, and that made it funnier than ever.

"What are you laughing at, Susie?" said Elsie.

"I don't know."

But she did. I knew. I can still see the hurt on her face.

"That's all right, Susie, we weren't laughing at you. We're just pretending." Then to Elsie, "Let's pretend to buy something for Susie. If she went shopping with us, we'd have to buy her *something.*"

"I guess."

"We have to buy her something before we quit. Susie, what would you like? I mean, If we really had the money, what would you like us to buy for you?"

Susie didn't know what to say. She never had any money.

"Just one thing, Susie. What would you like?"

She pushed her hair out of her eyes, looked down to the ground, then quickly up again. "Could I have two things?"

"Sure, Susie. You can have two things."

"Shoes? Could I have two shoes?"

"Sure. Sure. Patent leather, with straps and pearl buttons."

Susie pushed her hair back, her eyes as round as saucers. And blue. If her mother would comb her hair back she could even be pretty. *Next time we're out I'll comb Susie's hair.*

Elsie was already moving ahead. "That's all for you, Susie," she was saying. But "that's all" was enough; Susie was again prancing and twirling.

By this time we were approaching the tunnel.

"Shall we go in?"

"Yeah."

The tunnel proved more exciting than the outside. When you shouted, your voice bounced back – and back – and back, until you could barely hear it. Then again: "WHOO – WHOO – WHOO – whoo – oo – o. WHO CARES ABOUT SCHOO – OO – ool."

We had just about made it through the tunnel when we heard another train whistle. Soon came the engine, the black smoke, the train cars, and again we stood straight and still and watched the cars go by, singing out the names:

> "CHICAGO, MILWAUKEE and SAINT PAUL,"
> "THE BURLINGTON and THE MISSOURI,"
> "THE CANADIAN EXPRESS,"
> "THE GREAT NORTHERN,"
> "THE PENNSYLVANIA."

I never saw Susie so happy.

After we had waved to the man in the caboose, after we stood in silence listening to the last woo-woo, again, we didn't know what to do. "What shall we do now?"

"Let's see where the path goes."

"Okay." Elsie went first. The path began to turn upward, through weeds, through bramble. Something squawked and we jumped. Continuing. All at a once a clearing. With sheer delight we ran into the open space. Then I heard a *squeal*.

"A snake," squealed Elsie. I squealed. Susie squealed. Together we jumped into the weeds.

"What shall we do now?"

"I don't know."

Scared. Scared.

"Look," cried Susie. "Another path."

"Let's go."

We did.

"Maybe this is an Indian trail."

"Maybe there are Indians hiding."

Suddenly the path ended. We were standing on the edge of a hill, just the sky above, and down, down, down as far as you could see, were the railroad yards: engines, box cars, and little men working in and out like ants.

"How small they are!"

"And we, so big!"

I tried measuring one of the men between my thumb and forefinger; I couldn't get a space small enough. My hand covered the whole railroad yard.

"Elsie, how big we are. As high as the sky."

"Yeah."

"Like it was all ours. The whole railroad."

"If we owned the whole railroad, we could buy anything and never have to go to school again."

"Let's pretend. What shall we buy?"

"Anything. The biggest thing in the world."

"We could buy a circus."

"And ride the merry-go-round, jump off, then jump right back on again."

"And me? Could I ride, too?" said Susie.

"Sure, Susie," we cried. "As many rides as you want," I added. I pictured Susie flying from horse to horse.

"Once I got sick on the merry-go-round," said Elsie.

"You did?"

"Yeah. Real sick."

"We could walk around. We could go into the tent to watch the show. Or. . . or. . . we could eat. All the hot dogs we wanted and drink all the root beer . . . ."

"And me, too?"

"Oh yes, Susie. All you wanted."

"I'm getting hungry right now," said Elsie. "Let's eat."

"Okay."

"Now," said Elsie.

"Okay."

With a leafy branch, Elsie began brushing off a stone. Susie and I did the same. Then she sat down. Susie and I did the same. When she opened her lunchbox, we did, too, but when she brought out a napkin and spread it on her lap, we just looked. I didn't have a napkin. Neither did Susie. And when Elsie unwrapped a sandwich and threw away a beautiful piece of waxed paper — just threw it away — Susie and I watched it float, like a white bird, down the hill.

Mama didn't know about waxed paper. All we had was old newspapers and they weren't even in English. Susie was already eating — bread and jelly. That's all her mother ever gave her.

I felt around in my box. *A pork chop.* Mama didn't know about lunchmeat, either. Elsie had boiled ham, I could see. She was pulling all the fat off and throwing it away. Then she began breaking the crusts off her bread and throwing them away, too. Susie picked one up and stuffed it into her mouth.

"Don't do that, Susie."

But Elsie wasn't paying any attention to her. She was busy unwrapping a piece of chocolate cake. With chocolate icing. Once Mrs. Murray made chocolate cake with chocolate icing. She gave Mama a piece. We all had some.

"Don't watch, Susie."

I gave Susie some of my gingersnaps. Elsie didn't want any. But she gave us some of her orange. I had an apple. Elsie didn't want any. I gave cobs to Susie, and when Elsie wasn't looking I gave her my pork chop.

Then we heard a noise like somebody coming. As fast as we could scramble, we hid.

"Maybe an Indian," said Elsie, but it was only a railroad man. Without even looking around, he began to do Number One.

"Don't look," I mouthed to Susie.

Susie squeezed her eyes shut, but you could hear him plain as day. When he left, we tip-toed out.

"Okay Susie. You can open your eyes now."

"Once I saw our Georgie peein'."

"Susie!"

"I did, too. Once he peed all over me and Mama gave him a beatin'."

"Su-SIE!" I was never so embarrassed in my whole life. I could hear Elsie trying not to laugh. "Let's get out of here," I said, *before Susie says anything more.* But she did.

Coming close to me, she whispered: "Annie, I hafta p. . . p. . . I hafta Number One."

"Susie!"

"I do. I do. Right now." With these words, she quickly ran behind a clump of bushes. I thought I'd die, hoping Elsie didn't notice. English people didn't do that. But as soon as Susie returned, she went up.

I did, too.

Then we left.

Back in the tunnel we resumed our calling and yelling, the tunnel walls echoing and re-echoing, and when we emerged at the other end, we again began to skip along the railroad ties, until we came to a switch shanty.

"Let's go inside."

"Okay."

I peeked. Nobody. Behind the door, on a bench, where I knew it would be, was a pail of water with a dipper.

"I'm thirsty."

"Me, too."

We took turns drinking, then looked around. There was a table, a potbelly stove, some benches, raincoats hanging from a nail, and cigarette butts all over the floor.

"Let's clean up."

"Okay. I sweep," said Elsie.

"I dust."

"Me, too?"

"Here's a piece of waste." ("Waste" was the term used for wadded balls of thread used by railroaders for dusting and wiping.) "You can do the window sills."

"Okay."

Elsie, holding the broom, was trying to get my attention. There, on the inside of the door, was a picture of a girl. *Naked.*

"Don't look, Susie." Susie had seen Elsie motioning to me. "Don't look," I repeated. She backed away, a hurt look on her face.

"She's so. . . so innocent," I whispered to Elsie, the phrase more in the way of absolvement than in explanation. Once, out on the playground — Susie was just standing around as always — I heard Miss Mellon use those words to describe her — "so innocent" — and I liked it. The words made Susie almost likable. "So innocent," I repeated as we pushed the door back against the wall.

I knew about things like that. Once I was peeking into Uncle

Fedor's closet and saw a picture of a naked girl on the door, and closed it, never to look again.

"Girls aren't supposed to look at pictures like that," I said to Elsie.

That settled, we began what girls are supposed to do, Elsie sweeping the floor, Susie rubbing away at the window sills, and I to clearing the table. Silently, importantly, I began to hum. Susie followed. Then I stopped. Voices, Men talking. Then a crunch of footsteps coming closer and closer. Then two railroaders standing in the doorway.

"We-we're j-just c-cleaning up."

"I'm sweeping," said Elsie.

"Why aren't you girls in school?" said one of the men.

"B-because . . . ."

"Do your mothers know you're here?"

"N—no."

"Don't you know it's dangerous for little girls to be out like this?"

"N—no. I mean y—yes."

"You could be arrested."

Arrested?

"Ever been in jail?"

Jail? I didn't want to go to jail. I wanted to get out of there, but my lunchbox was on the bench behind the door and the scowly man was standing there and . . . .

The scowly man began reaching into his pocket. "Here," he said. "A dime for each of you. For cleaning up."

A dime for each of us! One for Elsie! One for Susie! And one for me! "M-mister, we'll c-come again. We'll c– come tomorrow. We'll c-come . . . ."

"You come here once more, young lady, I'll strap you." And he meant it.

"No," cried Susie, running out the door.

"Your lunchbox, Susie."

She ran back, picked up her lunchbox, then bolted out the door. She knew what a strap meant. Elsie and I followed.

"Make sure you all go straight home," the men had called to us.

"We will." But the dimes! We couldn't believe we each had a dime.

"How much is a dime, Annie?" whispered Susie.

"Same as two nickels," said Elsie.

"Like two pennies?"

"Susie. A dime is the same as *ten pennies*. TEN, Susie," I said to her. The amount astounded even me. "What shall we do, Elsie?"

"We could see a moving picture."

"How much will that cost?"

"A nickel. With a nickel left over. For a nickel we can buy candy. A full bag."

"Me too, Annie?"

"You too, Susie."

"Let's go," said Elsie.

And we did: across the yards, straight to Pitcairn, straight to Geraci's candy store, where we saw licorice strips with candy dots, little black babies, a cupful for a penny, pink and yellow caramels, three for a penny. Tootsie Rolls. Sourballs. And peanuts. If there ever was a Heaven on earth, it was Geraci's candy store.

Finally, after the candy man scolded, "I don't have all day," we were leaving the store, each clasping a precious bag of candy.

"Now we can go to the Strand," said Elsie. She knew where to go. She and her brother often went to the movies. Her father was a brakeman, and a brakeman made lots of money.

The Strand was next to the five and ten. I often looked at the signs on the outside, at pictures of movie stars, never dreaming that someday I'd be going inside. "Perils of Pauline," said a sign.

"Five cents," said a voice at the window. We each placed a nickel on the counter.

"This way," said Elsie.

I had never been to a moving picture show, so thrillingly dark, so tingly with excitement. Down, down, the aisle we went, Elsie first, then me, then Susie.

"Hold on to me, Susie."

"Okay."

We found seats. Sat down. "Right here, Susie."

"Okay."

"Save your candy, Susie."

"Okay."

"Look up there. Look at Pauline."

"Okay."

Pauline had just fallen into a sharp bramble, was getting up, her dress almost torn off. But she had to run. Wild men on wilder horses were chasing her. Getting closer and closer. Again she fell.

"Run, run, run," we yelled, stomping our feet, and again she fell. Almost over a cliff, but she didn't fall over. Holding on, she rolled under a rock, and *every horse, to the very last one, jumped right over the rock*. They didn't know she was there.

To this day I'll never know what happened to Pauline. On the screen, in large letters, flashed: "COME BACK NEXT WEEK FOR THE NEXT THRILLING CHAPTER." It was over. We had to go.

But Susie was asleep — clutching her candy and sleeping. She didn't even see the show. But I could tell her. I could tell her everything. That's when I heard Elsie saying something.

"What did you say, Elsie?"

"We could see the show again if we want to."

"Again? We can?"

"Yes. That's what we do. When we come, Mama says to see the show twice. Shall we? We don't have to pay."

"Susie, we can see the show again!" Susie was peeking into her candy bag.

"Okay," she said.

The second time was better than the first: We saw Keystone Kops, then some news, and then again, "PERILS OF PAULINE." And when it was over, Susie was asleep again, clutching her candy bag and asleep.

"Wake up, Susie."

When we got outside, *it was dark.*

Through the streets we ran, over the bridge, across the railroad yards and over the hump, as if by running we could, by some miracle, overtake the daylight. When we got to our house, all the lights were on and people all around.

"Your mother, too," I said to Elsie.

"I know."

After a barrage of "Thank Gods," after a few nips of "You should all be whipped," after everybody went home, after I had shared my candy with Mary and Mikie, after I was finally in bed, after accepting the fact that again I disappointed Pap, the scene slowly began to drift away. I fell asleep.

Sometimes a punishment seems more like a reward. Elsie and I had to stay after school for two weeks to clean the blackboards, and that was better than playing hooky: Just Elsie and I doing the blackboards, and then just Elsie and I, together, going home from school.

As for Susie? Sometimes things happen that even time cannot obliterate. *Somebody took her candy.* I can still see her standing at our kitchen door the following morning.

"Somebody took it, Annie."

The Pledge

The phrase, "If nothing is happening, something surely will," was never more true than one evening at our house.

For some reason, neither Aunt Julie nor Aunt Liza came down. Maybe that was why the men didn't come down either; they were upstairs in their own tobacco-filled world, the sound of their voices drifting down like muffled drums. Mama was salting the pork for next morning's breakfast and Pap was setting the lunch buckets in order. I had been reading a story until the kids fell asleep and was still holding the book, waiting for Mama to say, "Take them to bed already," when, in the silence, we began to hear a sound like crying.

They heard too — Pap already sighing, Mama's eyes turning heavenward. And they were right. The Donelkos again. Georgie was already pushing the door open and crying.

"Our Pap. He's drunk."

Behind him came Mikie, then Susie, then Mrs. Donelko, holding Pauly.

The outburst took no time to settle down; this had happened before. Their Mikie ran to our Mikie, Susie ran to me, Pauly, after his mother set him down, undecided then decided, ran to the boys. Our Mary joined Susie and me, and Georgie, still standing near the door had no place to go. But that didn't fool me. He'd be up to something soon.

The first thing Mama did was go to the pantry for bread and a jar of elderberry jelly. That's all it took, and the party was on, the kids already at the table, their exuberance exploding like firecrackers. Mama couldn't cut the bread fast enough.

"Something told me to bake today."

Pap was trying to quiet Mrs. Donelko, at the same time scolding the boys. Some bread had fallen to the floor, then as quickly, snapped up.

As soon as the table was cleared of all the food, the fun began: the boys began knocking each other around. Their Mikie pushed our Mikie, our Mikie hit his head on the edge of the table, Mrs. Donelko whacked their Mikie on his head, and when both babies began to cry, Pap reached for his belt. "Marsch. Time for bed."

Going to bed was even more fun: The girls got the bedroom and the boys got the *perina* on the kitchen floor, but no matter how hard we tried, we couldn't stop giggling.

"The men have to sleep," begged Mama.

What they didn't know was that every time it finally became quiet, Georgie Donelko would sneak into our bedroom and tickle our toes. Not until Pap cracked his belt against the door frame did the boys finally behave.

But it was exciting. Susie snuggled close to me. "I like coming here," she whispered. "I like sleeping here."

"Yeah. Me too."

"Maybe we can come again tomorrow."

"Yeah. Maybe your father will get drunk again."

Sleep descended on the household like a blessing, stayed the night, and when morning began to peek into the window, the quiet exploded like popcorn. The first thing I heard was Mrs. Donelko's voice: "*Cicho*" (Quiet).

I nudged Susie. "They're up." That awakened Mary. Together we slid out of bed, slid down the banister and tip-toed into the kitchen. The boys were being herded into Mama's bedroom where the baby was still sleeping.

"*Cicho*," pleaded Mama this time.

Pap had already built the fire in the stove and had gone to Donelkos'. Mama was busy with the lunches. After handing us a wet washcloth and towel, Mrs. Donelko went to help Mama, but we couldn't keep quiet. "Who took the washcloth?"

"You're hogging the towel."

"Mama, he pushed me again."

Both babies began to cry. I went to our baby, Susie to theirs. Uncle Fedor took care of the boys. The men were beginning to come down. Mrs. Donelko was helping Mama.

By the time the men had eaten and left for work, we were already lined up for morning prayers, then to the table to eat: bread dipped in hot pork drippings then spread with mustard. Again, Mama couldn't cut the bread fast enough, saying for the umpteenth time, "Something told me to bake."

Pap returned from the Donelkos.

"*Dobre* [Good]," was his report. He picked up his bucket and left.

"*Slava Bohu*," sighed Mrs. Donelko. She began herding her kids together. It being Saturday, nobody had to go to school, so nobody had to hurry. As they left, I called to Susie, "See you later." She loved it when I said that.

Later came sooner than expected. Uncle Mike was wiping his face with a towel, Mama was picking up a crumb from the table, waiting for Uncle Mike to finish, so she could tell him all that had happened, when a knock came at the door. It was Susie.

"What's the matter, Susie?"

"Our pap. He wants to go to church. To Saint Aloysius. To swear. Our mother said, Could Annie come, too?"

I was ready immediately. Susie and I were with him one other time when he went to Father Sandor to swear.

"So now he wants to go to the Irish church. What's the matter with our church?" said Uncle Mike.

Mama said, "*Nye prialoshe*" [It didn't take].

"And in the Irish Church it will take? Father McGary can't keep his own Irish from drinking, how can he help one of us?"

"Let him go," said Mama. "It can't hurt."

That's how, for the second time, Susie and I and Mr. Donelko were going to a priest to swear off drinking, this time walking to Wilmerding, to St. Al's — no sidewalks, mud road, with Susie's flippety soles getting stuck and Mr. Donelko moaning, "Oi, oi."

By the time we got to Wilmerding where the road was paved, there was more mud on our shoes than there was on the road.

"Wipe your shoes, Susie," I said, then "wipe your nose."

I don't know why she was crying.

By the time we got to the priest's house the mud was almost all off, but just the same, because of the nice clean rug, I cautioned, "Don't step on the rug, Susie."

"Okay."

Mr. Donelko was knocking on the door.

A lady in a dust cap appeared in the doorway.

One startled look and she would have closed the door on us if Mr. Donelko hadn't put his foot in the doorway.

"I vant it priist," he said, very politely, "I vant it svare."

Again the lady tried to close the door, and again Mr. Donelko wouldn't let her, saying again, "I vant it priist."

A voice from the inside called, "Who is it?"

It was Father McGary. He came to the door and looked at us.

"Fah-dare, I vant it svare. By oltar I vant it."

Father McGary said nothing. Maybe he didn't understand. I began stammering. "H—he, h—he, M—Mr. D—Donelko, h—he was d—drunk, an—an . . . ."

"And he wants to take the oath. Is that it?"

"Y—yes," I said. "The o—oath."

"No-no-no-no-no," cried Mr. Donelko. "No oats. Juus svare."

"*To jedno*," [the same], I explained. "Oath — swear."

Father McGary looked at Mr. Donelko and frowned, but when he looked at Susie and me, he smiled. "Come with me," he said.

We followed Father McGary down the steps then into the church, and nobody there. I was never in a church with nobody there. So dim and quiet. So holy. Just a few candles away down on the altar, and that's where we went. To the altar.

Father McGary began to pray — began to say, "Repeat after me," but Mr. Donelko didn't know the language, so Father McGary did the praying himself, asked Mr. Donelko to kneel, prayed some more, then asked Mr. Donelko to rise.

"Go and drink no more," he said, and I just knew by the tears in Mr. Donelko's eyes that he would never ever take another drink.

And when we all went to pray before the Blessed Mother, to watch over all widows and orphans and men lost at sea, he didn't add:

> And for me, Dear Lady, if you'd be so good,
> A drink or two. I know you could.

When we got home, Mama was happy, Mrs. Donelko was happy.

"Maybe this time, it will work," said Uncle Mike.

For awhile it did. Mr. Donelko began fixing his sidewalks, began chopping his own kindling wood — Georgie didn't have to come borrowing — and dug a little garden. "We won't have to come down for parsley anymore," said Mrs. Donelko. He began going to church again.

Then, one evening, Mama was salting the pork for next morning's breakfast, the kids had fallen asleep on the floor, I was holding a book, falling asleep myself, when, in the silence, we began to hear a sound like crying.

You'll Be Beautiful Forever

It was Saturday. I had just finished scrubbing the last things: the outside toilet, then the sidewalks, when Mama called to me. "To the store. I need soup bones."

"Okay, Mummie." Sometimes I called her "Mummie." That's what Ella May called her mother, 'Mummie.' "Can I change my dress?"

"Yes, but hurry."

"I will." With one last swipe, I placed the broom against the wall to dry, then ran upstairs to the dress closet where I reached at once for my very best dress, the new one with the violets. Because Frankie would be there. He worked on Saturdays.

All the girls loved Frankie. I did, too, but he liked only Caroline. Just the same I wanted to look nice. Quickly, I combed my hair, this way, no, that way, then ran downstairs.

"What? Your new dress? Is this Sunday?"

Upstairs again. Changed into another dress I had already worn to church. And all the way to the store I prayed.

"Please, God, for just one minute, make me beautiful."

Every night I offered extra "Our Fathers" and extra "Hail Marys" to make me beautiful and nothing happened, but this time? All I wanted was one minute. He could do it. "Please, please."

Once inside the store I saw Frankie right away. He was at the back doing something with boxes, his head bobbing up and down, up and down, his hair falling forward and he tossing his head backward just the way I did when both my hands were busy, and all I did was toss my head and didn't know Mr. Hessler had been calling me.

"Annie, are you deaf? I don't have all day."

I jumped. The next thing I knew I was sprawled on the floor, my money somewhere in the sawdust.

That night I didn't pray at all. *If that's how HE was going to be.* Not the next night either. And when I sang to the baby, not one holy song. Then one day, something else happened.

It was so hot you couldn't even breathe. All day long the baby just cried and cried until Mama couldn't stand it any more. "Call Mrs. Murray," she said to me.

Mrs. Murray knew everything: how to make a poultice if you had a cold, how to fix a broken leg – all you had to do was wrap a flat board around the leg. If your arm was red and swollen, raw potatoes. When she looked at the baby, she knew.

"Just a rash. It's the heat," she said, rocking the baby in her arms. "A little talcum powder and she'll be all right. Send Annie to the five and ten."

I was ready. "Like a soldier," Uncle Mike once said.

Mama tied two dimes into the corner of a handkerchief. "And don't lose it," she said, pushing the handkerchief into my fist. "Now run."

"I won't. I will."

She didn't have to tell me to run. I loved going to the five and ten. So many things to see: rings and beads and bracelets and pictures of movie stars.

Once inside, I went straight to the pictures. Tom Mix, Mary Pickford, Lillian Gish. I could have looked at Lillian Gish forever — so sad. Sometimes I tried looking sad to see if somebody would notice but no one ever did.

That's when I saw all those ladies: They were grouped together, all looking at a man, listening to him. I went to see. The man was holding a jar high in his hand.

"This little jar," he was saying, "this Miracle Clay, holds beauty secrets once known only to ancient beauties of Egypt. But it's not a secret any more. Now these ingredients can be found on the dressing tables of our own beauties of stage and screen."

I pushed my way to the front.

"But the biggest miracle of all is that what once could not be purchased at any price can now be had for only pennies. One quarter, and you, too, can be beautiful forever."

One quarter. I had a quarter. The one I found in the post office. It was at home under the Blessed Mother. And I had a nickel in my shoe: the one Uncle Mike gave me for getting him tobacco.

My mind went into action: Buy the Miracle Clay, run home, get my quarter, run back for the talcum powder. I untied the two dimes, got the nickel out of my shoe, and waited my turn.

"Smart little girl," the man said.

All the way home I prayed that Mrs. Murray would still be there so Mama wouldn't notice. But she wasn't.

Mama was busy at the table making noodles and the baby was still crying and Uncle Mike was trying to quiet her, but he didn't know the right way to hold her. He didn't even know the right songs to sing.

Mama said, "What took you so long?"

Walking sideways, I dropped my package into an opened drawer, reached for the baby, then went to the rocking chair to sing, but Mama had seen. Already she was taking my package out of the drawer.

"Rock-a-bye-baby, on the tree top," I began to sing.

Now she was taking the jar out of the bag.

"What?" she asked, handing the jar to Uncle Mike.

"*When the wind blows, the cradle will rock.*"

Uncle Mike examined the jar.

"Nothing. Nothing" he said. "Something for – for face. Nothing."

That's when Pap came in.

"*When the bough breaks, the cradle will fall.*"

"See what your Hancha do? I send her to store to bring baby powder and she bring this – this –"

"*Down will come cradle, baby and all.*"

"Nothing, nothing," said Uncle Mike. "Something for face. For ladies."

"For ladies? For face?"

One other time I saw that look on Pap's face: the time I found a jar somewhat like Miracle Clay in the dump and brought it home and Uncle Fedor laughed. "For ladies," he said, "for face," but he didn't say "ladies." He used that bad word.

And now Uncle Mike was saying, "For ladies. For face."

With one quick swipe, Pap grabbed the jar, went to the still open door, and threw it as far as it would go. *Please, God, don't let it go too far. Not as far as the dump.*

That evening, after dishes, after everyone had settled down, after Aunt Julie and Aunt Liza and the others came, I sneaked the instructions into my apron, went into the cellar, then out. The jar wasn't anywhere in the yard. It wasn't on the street. The dump. That's where it had to be, and there it was, on top of some cans. *Thank you, God.* I swooped it up, flew across the street, through the yard, and into the cellar, then stopped to listen.

Aunt Liza was telling a funny story and everybody was laughing. *Please don't stop, Aunt Liza.*

I reached for the matches on the windowsill, lit the kerosene lamp, opened the pamphlet, and began to read: "Spread gently over the face. Wait three minutes, then, very gently, rinse off with cool water." *That's all. Only three minutes.*

Upstairs, they were still talking and laughing. *Please, Aunt Liza make them laugh.* Quickly I opened the jar, dipped my fingers into the clay and began to spread it over my cheeks, over my forehead, over my nose. All over. Then a little over my left eye. Maybe the cream could straighten my left eye. Then the count.

But I didn't have a clock. Then I remembered: Ten "Hail Marys," properly recited, took almost three minutes.

I began to pray slowly, properly. Already I could feel the beauty working.

Then the baby began to cry. And I was only on the seventh Hail Mary. *Hurry, hurry. Please stop crying. Hurry.*

I made it, only to discover: *no water.* Not in the tub, not in the watering can, not anywhere and now the baby was screaming.

"ANNIE," I heard Mama call.

That's when I heard the door to the cellar open. *Oh, Blessed Mother, help me.* Quickly, I tried to blow out the light. But it wouldn't go out. Pap was halfway down the steps, Mikie right after him, and when Mikie saw me he yelled, "Annie's here. Our Annie's here. She's all over mud. Her face is all over mud."

Then came Aunt Julie. Then Mama with the baby. Then Georgie sliding on his hind end. Then all of them, like statues, looking at me. Aunt Julie began to laugh, but Pap stopped her.

"*Cicho,*" he said. Taking the baby from Mama he said to her, "Wash her face." To the others, "Upstairs," and they went.

Later, after everyone was in bed, I looked into the mirror. Nothing. If only the baby hadn't started to cry, if only I had had time to say the "Hail Marys" properly, if only . . . if only . . . if only . . . . Suddenly I thought of something. *I hadn't used up all the clay.* I could start all over again.

Very slowly I began to tip-toe out of the room, then down the steps — remembering to skip the ones that creaked, when, through the railings, I saw a light. It came from the kitchen, and there was Mama, at the kitchen table, *spreading clay over her face.*

Princess for a Day

It has been said that Eve lost paradise when she first became aware that life was not fair.

There was Adam, talking only to God, and there was God talking only to Adam, and when the two decided upon inviting the Angel Gabriel to Eden for a visit, who did all the work? Eve did. First she had to walk all over Eden gathering the ripest of the fruit, the plumpest of gourds, the juiciest of berries. From the berries she made dulcet creams. An ordinary cream just wouldn't do. Every concoction that Eden had to offer, she brought to her table. And when that was done, she spread the way with rose petals. It took John Milton forty-nine lines of poetry in *Paradise Lost* to tell it. What did Adam do? Adam went to greet the guest.

And when the party was over — when Angel Gabriel had to leave, Adam went with him. Eve was left alone to clean up the mess. Is it any wonder that when the serpent came slithering into Eden, Eve was a ready victim. Why wouldn't she eat the apple? Nobody told her anything. All God did was talk to Adam.

That's how matters were then; that's how matters are now. Everybody paid attention to Mikie because he was a boy, and to Mary. Mary was the pretty one — always laughing — making everybody laugh. That is why Mama didn't blame Mary for the baby falling down the stairs.

And I told Mary to watch the baby. All I wanted to do is read one more chapter, but Mary ran out to play, and the baby fell, and Mama caught me reading, and that is why I was blamed.

And I told her I was sorry. I really was. I didn't want the baby to get hurt. And now again. When she left for Rosary, I really meant to do the dishes.

"I will, I will," I said, but I had this book about a missing heiress I had borrowed from Becky Rubin; Ella Marie was next in line to read, so I had to hurry.

Poor heiress! The castle and everything in it belonged to her but nobody knew what had happened to her. She was stolen when a baby, and everybody thought she was somewhere in India, but she wasn't. She was right there in the kitchen, doing all the kitchen chores. Even she didn't know.

The proof was in a little tin box wrapped in a piece of old blanket and shoved under her very own cot in the attic. It was put there by a long-ago nurse. One stormy night, she had opened the door to a wretched lady holding a little baby. She handed the baby to the nurse, gave her the packet, then quickly disappeared.

The baby was taken in, the package shoved under the cot. When the old nurse died, the packet was forgotten, but the little girl stayed on in the big house. When she was old enough, she was placed in the kitchen, scolded by everybody because she was a nobody. If they only knew. Chapter after chapter, page after page, and still nobody knew. Even she didn't know.

I was reading the book when I heard the gate slam. *Mama. She was back.* And the dishes were still all over the table.

A few swoops and everything was in the pan; when Mama walked into the kitchen I was pouring hot water and singing her favorite hymn, "Hail, Holy Queen." Nothing.

Heartened, I raised my voice to its fullest, I was going into the good part: "My pro-tec-tor-ress," when I heard a sound like paper tearing.

The book! Mama was tearing up Becky's book. And stuffing it into the fire. I had forgotten to hide it. Only a lazy girl reads books. I knew that.

"Mama!"

She didn't even hear me.

"Mama, it's not mine. The book isn't mine." I began grabbing at what remained of the book, an unheard-of thing to do, when Pap walked in.

"What, already?"

"What? The devil, that's what." Then she started: about how, after Rosary, Father Sandor came into talk to the ladies about the devil and how he works.

"Are your children reading books?" he asked. "Do you know what they are? Do you look at the pictures? Fancy ladies. Destroy them. They are the work of the devil himself."

"The devil? In books?" Pap was proud of my reading. Proud of my English. "What harm could there be?"

" 'Lest their heads be filled with evil thoughts and their hearts with wickedness.' That's what Father Sandor said."

"Just ten years old, she is," said Pap.

"Eleven." I corrected him, as if being eleven entitled me to read. But the book was already in the stove.

When Uncle Mike walked in he agreed with Mama. "Father Sandor is right. It's the devil's work to put a book into the hands of a little girl. Always was and always will be. The oldest of the old knew that. Educate a girl, you'll have a shrew for a wife."

That's when I became really certain about something that had been on my mind for a good while. Uncle Mike was not my real uncle, and Mama was not my real mother. That's why she burned the book. So I wouldn't know. That's why I had to do all the work. Who knows what was in her bag when she came from the Old Country? Maybe me.

I finished the dishes. Because the baby was playing, I went upstairs where I had another book, but I didn't read. I was now plotting my own story: I didn't really belong to this family.

But what could I do? Back down before she starts hollering again. With great reluctance I walked down the stairs, then into the kitchen. Everybody eating and talking at one time. Nice people didn't do that. Nice people ate with their mouths closed. I couldn't possibly be one of them. And when it came my turn to eat — after the kids had eaten — I didn't. Not that kind of food. *Halushki.*

One day I heard Elizabeth Stansfield say to Mary Etta that they were having a casserole for dinner. A *casserole*? I didn't know what that was but my mouth began to water anyway, so I must have known something.

The next morning I again decided not to eat, but did she notice? "Hurry or you'll be late," then, "Tie up the lunches." At the last moment I decided not to take mine. Just leave it on the table. *Then what would she say?*

Outside, Susie was already waiting for me. I ignored her. She ran ahead to join some other girls but they ignored her too, so she ran back to walk with me.

Sometimes they didn't talk to me either, but this morning it didn't matter. Wait until they found out I wasn't really me, not really Annie. I began to wonder: What really was my name? *Maybe Yolanda. Yes, Yolanda.* In one of the books there was a beautiful Yolanda.

Now that I had a name, it was easy to pretend.

All day at school I didn't raise my hand, not even once. I wasn't one of them. And when we were marching out, Miss Mellon asked if I was feeling well. "You look a little pale," she said.

"I do?"

As soon as I got home I went straight to the mirror to look, and I did look pale. That was more proof. All princesses were pale. And if I didn't eat my supper, maybe I'd even faint. Princesses fainted a lot. Then what would they say?

Mama didn't even notice that I wasn't eating, didn't even notice that Mary and Mikir were gobbling up all the food. And when the food was gone, after they had eaten it all, she said to me, "Diapers. Don't forget the diapers." *And I hadn't eaten yet.*

Quickly I grabbed the last piece of bread out of Mikie's hand, shoved it into my mouth, picked up the diaper pail and headed for the pump, Mikie screaming after me.

"She took my bread. Annie took my bread."

That did it. Never would I be Annie again. With the tips of my fingers, I picked out a diaper by its tippy end and began, distastefully, to swish it back and forth, back and forth.

"What are you doing, Annie?" called Mama from the porch.

What was I doing? As if she cared.

After diapers, after they were hanging on the line, she did say, "My, how nice they look." Then I had to go to the store. Because I could run fast, but I didn't run. I walked. Princesses didn't run, and if the girls on the way to the store asked me to jump rope with them, I wouldn't. Princesses didn't jump rope either.

But nobody was around. Just me walking alone to the store, sad and alone, the way princesses walked, and when I got to the store I didn't just run in and say, "Mama needs some barley." I waited for Mr. Gilchrist to wait on me.

"Mama needs some barley," I said sadly.

"Are you all right?" he asked.

What did he know?

He handed me the barley. I thanked him, kindly and sadly. He noticed; there was a certain something in his eye. *Maybe he, too, suspected.* Mr. Gilchrist was no dummy.

I began to run, then stopped myself. When I got home, Mama asked, "What took you so long?"

Later, after I had washed the kids, I went out to sit on the porch. To be alone. Mary Etta and them were beginning to jump rope. I thought of joining them. Sometimes they asked me to jump with them; sometimes they didn't. After thinking about it, I decided to go down. If they asked me to jump, I'd just say, "No, thank you."

But they didn't ask.

That's when I saw Susie running down the alley — probably saw me standing there — probably thought the girls would ask her to jump rope. But they didn't. They never did, she in those long dresses and flip-floppy soles, always tripping and crying, "Oh, I missed."

We stood there for a while just watching, she on one side and I on the other, until the girls grew tired. With a chorus of "Good-nights" and "See you tomorrows." they separated. Then there was only Susie and me.

I could tell she wanted to come over to where I was standing, maybe to talk. I called to her.

"Wanna come over?"

"Sure," she said, looking toward her house, then darting across the space between us.

All the way up to our house we talked about mothers, how they are, then just before turning into our yard, I asked her, "Susie, do you ever have thoughts? You know, about how our mothers came from the Old Country and all? We really don't know much about them, do we? Anything could have happened. Like in novels. Remember my telling you? About babies being kidnapped, and all?"

"Oh, yes. All the time. And you know something, Annie? I don't think my mother is my real mother."

Don't Tell

Once I became a seventh grader, I just had to tell Susie not to walk with me anymore. Not even come to our house anymore. "Can't you see I'm too big for you? You're only in the sixth grade."

"That's almost seventh."

To get to seventh you had to run up those wide, wide stairs, like going to Heaven, and this morning Mary Etta ran with me, and if Susie had tagged along, maybe she wouldn't have. "Don't follow me anymore, Susie."

Susie backed away, looking at me. And that evening she was back again, standing outside the kitchen door, afraid to come in.

"Susie," I began in my most scolding voice, but before I could say another word, she stuck out her hand.

"Here, Annie. A piece of candy."

"Candy? W—where d—did you—?"

Just then we heard Georgie running down the alley, yelling, "You're gonna get it, Susie, just you wait," but before he leaped through the gate Susie was already gone, and when Georgie got there, we didn't know which way she went.

"What happened?" I asked.

"She took my candy."

Later that evening, after Georgie Donelko had made a second trip to our house looking for Susie, I thought to go outside and look around. I heard a sound from behind the lilac bushes, like somebody calling my name.

"Susie, what are you doing there?"

All she said was "Annie." I reached out my hand but she wouldn't move.

"Susie, what's wrong?"

"I can't tell you, Annie," she whispered. "I can't tell nobody."

"Can't you even come out of there?"

I had to *pull* her out, then asked again, "What's wrong with you? Did you get a beatin'?"

"I can't tell you. I can't tell nobody."

"Susie, I'll shake you." I would have, too, but she was already shaking so hard I had to hold her up.

"Annie, don't holler at me."

"I'm not hollering at you, Susie, but we can't just stand here. If you don't tell me, I'll have to leave you."

"Don't leave me, Annie."

"Then tell me what's wrong. Let's go over to the steps." We did. "Now tell me. Where were you?"

"O—over – o—over—"

"Where, over?"

"O—over M—Mr. A—Adamson."

"Why did you go there, Susie?"

"I—I d—don't know. I was just walking, when . . . ."

"When what?"

"He said he had some candy."

"Candy?"

"Yes. He said to come inside. He said if I came inside he would give me more candy."

"Did you go?"

"Y—Yes. I didn't want to, Annie, but he s—said he had l—lots of candy."

"Did he give you some?"

"Y…yes. He said if I sat down he would give me more."

"Did he?"

"I can't tell you, Annie."

"Well, if you can't, you can't. But we can't sit here all night, either."

I began to walk away but she grabbed my hand.

"Annie, don't leave me. Don't leave me." She began shaking again, and again. I had to hold her.

"Then tell me."

"I will. I will. Just don't go away."

"Okay."

"Remember, one time, you and Bridget were talking. You told me to go away, but I didn't. I listened. About what men do to women. That's what he did. H—he kissed my mouth then th—threw me on the bed and tied me and he did it. Then again he did it. And it hurt. He said if I told he'd steal our baby. Don't tell, Annie. Don't tell."

"Oh, Susie. I won't. I won't. I'll never tell. Steal your baby? What'll we do?"

"Just don't leave me."

"But you have to go home, Susie. It's nighttime. Your Georgie was looking for you a long time ago. Your mother doesn't know where you are. You might get a beatin'."

"I'm afraid, Annie."

"I'll go with you, okay? Then maybe your mother won't hit you. Okay? Then on Sunday — on Sunday, Susie, we'll take a long walk. Just you and me. A long walk. And we'll talk. Just the two of us. Okay, Susie?"

But Susie did get a beatin'. I could her screams all the way back to the house.

The next morning, Georgie came running down for Mama. He said Susie had been screaming all night "and nobody was even hitting her. But now she's quiet. Mama said for you to come right away."

Then they called Mrs. Murray, and Mrs. Murray said to call the doctor, but when the doctor came, Susie wouldn't let him touch her – – just screamed and screamed — so they called the priest, and he held the Blessed Host over her head. Then she fell asleep.

But at night she screamed again, as soon as she fell asleep, and if somebody just touched her, she shrieked.

"It's the devil," said Mrs. Donelko.

One day Mrs. Donelko said for me to go up and I did. Susie was sitting up in bed, just staring. Didn't even know I was there.

When I left I ran all the way home. "Don't tell," she had said.

One day, Susie was taken away. "To a home for sick children," said Mama.

To Uncle Mike she said, "They had to tie her. We'll have to pray."

They had to tie her? The way Mr. Adamson did? I rushed up to my room and closed the door.

"Don't tell on me, Annie. Don't tell," she had said.

Every night, after we had finished our prayers, Mama would add, "And Susie. Take care of Susie."

Then came a day — I had just ran in from school — Mama said, "Susie isn't with us anymore. God took her."

When they brought her home, she was placed in a white coffin, dressed in a white dress and veil. Because she was still a virgin.

Little Julie, Little Liza, Bridget and I were her flower girls.

"An angel now," said Father Sandor. "She will live in Paradise forever."

An Accident

The things that were bestowed upon me simply because I was the eldest are countless; even if Mama were here a hundred years, as she once said, and had a hundred children, I would still have been the eldest; it would have been I, as soon as I was old enough, who got to do grown-up jobs like preparing Sunday dinners.

Church was St. Peter and Paul's in Braddock. And every Sunday a congregation of Byzantines walked across the Pitcairn Railroad Yards to the Pitcairn Railroad Station to board a train for Braddock. I can still hear them at the Station, everybody greeting everybody else, all talking at once, waiting for the train to come, then, once on the train, once settled in their seats, continuing without a break until they got to Braddock. Then after services, again, at the Braddock Station waiting for the train to bring them home again. It was two in the afternoon before everybody was back. Every Sunday, a pilgrimage.

That is why, as soon as I was old enough, I didn't have to go to Braddock; instead of turning left to go to the station, I continued straight ahead to St. Michael's Roman Catholic Church in Pitcairn. This way I was home by twelve with plenty of time to prepare Sunday dinner: pork chops with lots of onions and fried potatoes, the way Gavaj liked them. He ate before the others were back.

Always, when we left for church, I walked with Pap. Mama was with the other ladies, the kids with other kids, and Pap and I always together.

But this one Sunday, after saying "See you later, Pap," instead of continuing straight ahead toward St. Michael's, I stopped and looked back. And there was Pap, standing still, looking at me. It was a strange moment, as if we didn't want to part.

With an embarrassed wave of his hand, Pap waved me on.

"See you later, Pap," I said again.

An omen? Was something about to happen?

A few evenings after this, we were sitting in the kitchen, dishes done, the men upstairs, when Georgie Donelko burst into the kitchen crying.

"Our Pap. He's dead."

Mama gasped, "*O Hospodi*," threw a scarf over her shoulders and shot out the door, Georgie Donelko after her, Mary and Mikie after Georgie. I grabbed the baby to follow.

"No," she said. "You stay home. All of you." Then to me, "Watch the baby, watch the kids."

Watch the baby, watch the kids. Every time something good happened, I had to watch the baby, watch the kids. I watched from the window.

Through the yard and up the alley they went, first Mama, then Georgie, then nothing. Just Donelko's yard: the rusty pump, the broken sidewalk — Mr. Donelko never did have time to fix it — and their gate, swinging back and forth, back and forth, on its one hinge, as if in grief. No more would Mr. Donelko be staggering through.

I began to sniffle. Mary and Mikey looked at me. They never cried. They never had to. They never had to do anything.

But when evening came, we all got to go. The baby, too. Mama wrapped three loaves of bread in her apron and a jar of elderberry jelly. Mary took Georgie's hand, I carried the baby. Mikey strutted ahead.

When we got to the Donelkos — as soon as we opened the door, without even looking at each other, Mrs. Donelko and Mama began to wail. Without even disturbing them, someone took the food from Mama, and together they all went wailing into the front room. We followed.

The front room was all cleaned up, with clean curtains. No beds. The chairs were against the wall, then over against the side wall was the casket, Mrs. Donelko and Mama wailing over it, but when the babies began to cry, George and I had to take them into the kitchen. That's when Aunt Julie and Uncle Maksim came in.

Little Julie came straight to me, Uncle Maksim joined the men, and Aunt Julie, with one long wail, went into the next room. That gave Mama a chance to come into the kitchen. She didn't have to wail.

"Everybody into the kitchen," Mama ordered. "Everybody" meant only the kids, we knew that. The men were busy just talking and listening, and as soon as Mama sliced the bread and spread it with jelly, the kids all together were at the table.

More people came: Aunt Liza and Uncle Jakub and Little Liza. Uncle Jakub joined the men, Little Liza came to the table and Aunt Liza went into the front room. More men and more ladies and more kids, and that had to be the nicest moment I had ever experienced in the Donelkos' house: Aunt Julie and Aunt Liza taking turns wailing, the men listening, each proud of his wife's performance, and we, the kids, no fighting, no arguing, nobody hitting anybody, just busy eating bread and jelly and tea and listening.

The men didn't have to wait but all night long they took turns to sit with the cantor whose duty was to read the Psalters — those who could read relieving him now and then.

This was repeated on the second night. More people and more kids. This time Mama brought a huge pan of doughnuts. Mama always made doughnuts for funerals. The kids ate, the men talked quietly or just listened, the women wailed, each taking a turn, each asking Mr. Donelko to forgive them for a slight remembered:

for the time I laughed at you,
for the time I refused to help you,
for the many times I ignored you,
and on,
and on.

Aunt Julie, standing at the head of the coffin, taking Mr. Donelko's part, said:

Do not dwell on what was done.
Someday we will live as one,
For all eternity.

And when Mrs. Donelko began to cry, "Why did you have to leave me? Your children, now orphans," Aunt Julie's reply was:

Forgive me, my Zushka, for the many times I hurt you;
Forgive me, my children, for the many times I ignored you.

Aunt Julie was really good; better than even Aunt Liza. Aunt Liza was good for laughing, Aunt Julie good for crying. For once even Uncle Maksim bragged.

"From her mother she learn. In Old Country, when somebody die, they call her."

I didn't know where to stand: in the kitchen where the men were telling stories, or in the room where the women were wailing.

Next day was the funeral.

Morning came at once, Pap waking us. I jumped out of bed, straight to the wash basin, splashed water on my face, wiped my face dry and did the same to Georgie. Still in my petticoat, I dressed Georgie, then myself. When we got downstairs, the men were finished eating. It was our turn. So we wouldn't get food on our clothes, we ate standing up, bread with jelly and tea.

When we got to the Donelkos, their house was already filled with people. I could barely squeeze through. Holding Georgie's hand, I wiggled my way toward the coffin. Mama was at the back, holding the baby. Pap was already standing with the men. Aunt Julie and Aunt Liza were wailing, first one, then the other, then together, telling a story: "Why did you have to go? Your wife a widow now, your children orphans."

The Donelko kids were all huddled together beside their mother, who was rocking back and forth, back and forth, like their gate. Georgie looked very nice in a suit. Mrs. Murray let him wear their Jimmie's. He also had a nice haircut.

Mr. Donelko looked nice, too, in a suit and haircut. With his hands folded across his chest it almost didn't look like him, and again Aunt Julie, wailing for him, began, "Forgive me if I ever hurt you."

That made Mrs. Donelko cry out, "Why did you go?" Georgie began to sob.

Then somebody said, "The priest. He's here."

In the sudden silence was heard the scuffling of shoes, the rustle of robes, the clink of the censer. Uncle Maksim cleared the doorway.

And when the priest appeared, black robed, censer swinging, followed by the cantor, and when both began to sing, "*Blahosloven Boh nas*," the wailing began again.

". . . Because he hoped in Me," they sang, "I will fill him with the length of days and he shall not be afraid of the night."

I looked at Georgie and wondered, *How does it feel if your father is dead?*

I looked to where Pap was standing, and he was looking at me. He often did that. I did, too. Sometimes we had the same thoughts. Was he thinking the same thing: What if that was him in the coffin?

Sometimes I slipped something into his lunch bucket to surprise him, and I knew the exact moment he found it. And when he came home that night he always said, "I knew it was there."

Now he was looking at me. He wasn't singing "Lord have mercy."

I wasn't singing either. I tried, but my voice came out scratchy: A dreadful thought had passed between us.

Again I tried to make myself sing, "Have mercy, O Lord," but the words came out like crying.

The ladies were beginning to make moaning sounds, getting ready to wail, because now came the end. When the cantor began, "Rest the soul where neither pain or sorrow . . ." they began.

Now the priest was swinging the censer over the coffin, over the people, singing with the cantor, and through the incense, it wasn't

Mr. Donelko in the coffin. It was Pap. And when the priest and the cantor began to sing "*Vichnaja pamjat*," it was for him they sang.

"Don't cry, don't cry," somebody said, but I couldn't stop.

To this day, the crying hasn't stopped. Like a healing scar, I had to grow over and above that cry, because, it was Pap.

I had gotten to the gate first, to be ahead of the others when he came home from work, but he didn't come. All the other men came, but not Pap. Not anymore.

"It was an accident," someone said.

"The years were many, and the years were long," said the poet.

Where are they now?

The rising tones of the chants were beginning to draw me into the folds of the present; the priest, now at the most sacred point of the Mass was beginning to raise the Host. As one, all head bowed; too much for the eye to look upon.

"*PRIJMITE, JADITE*," began Father Anselm, "*SIJE JEST T'ILO MOJE, JEZE ZA VY LOMIMOJE.*"

Eat, this is my Body, broken for you, even as bread is broken before it is eaten — consume, until it becomes a part of you — as Pap and Mama are now a part of me, as is Susie, as is Aunt Julie, as is every being that ever had, that does now, that ever shall touch me.

My mind wandering, I think of those who left for a better place to live.

"Anyplace but here," was an oft-quoted remark.

Little Julie, married, lives in Scranton. Ironically, Aunt Julie never did experience the pride and joy of being the mother of the bride. Little Julie married after her mother had passed on.

Little Liza, a beauty like her mother, eloped with an Englishman and was never heard from. "High class now," was the comment.

The Donelkos, all, did well. Even Michael. Michael, the youngest, had been stricken with polio when a baby. A poor family has no place for such a handicap, but the wheels do grind. Came World War II. Because every able– bodied young man had been inducted into the Service, Michael was able to get work. They were glad to have him. Mrs. Donelko finally had some money in her purse.

"I never had it so good," she would say. "And to think, it is my Michael, the crippled one, who did this for me."

"Y . . . Yeah," Michael would add in his halting speech, "d—dey d—don't even c—come here anymore." His brothers, he was talking about.

Still, they loved him. When he died — when they got the word — they came. All of them.

> They all came, Michael,
> As soon as they got the word.
> All four of them.
> John, the eldest.

A son, an artist in New York.
Remember how he protected you?

George, the comedian. From California.
Has appeared on television.
Did you know that?
Remember how he made you laugh?

Joseph, the tough one.
A big farm. Cattle and everything.
They had to protect you from him.
But you loved being roughed up.

And Pauly, the youngest.
With the largest family. Five.
One in college.
For awhile he belonged to you.

For awhile there were just the two of you.
Then he, too, went away.

Then there was only you.

Busy. Everybody busy.

But they came.
When they got the word.
All four.

They stood before you like archangels,
Told their tales,
Then looked at you, and cried.

Ena's story became one of the sad ones. After the wedding, she and Michael went to Sharon where he had a job. For awhile, happiness. Within a year a little girl was born: Hanka.

But Michael began to develop health problems. Severe asthma. On the day that a second little girl was born, Michael was taken to a hospital and never recovered. Ena was left with two little girls. She began to look for housework. But two babies?

As if planned by an Unseen Power, help was on the way. Michael's younger brother, John, was already on the way to America. When he arrived, he also brought with him an extra pair of hands. He tended the babies while Ena went to work, and regularly, every few hours, took the little ones to Ena's place of employment to be nursed.

John fell in love with Ena. They married. Ena became a housewife again.

But Unseen Powers sometimes go berserk. Right after a son was born to the two, Ena became ill. Tuberculosis.

She struggled hard to live. Then she, too, died.

Following came a tangled mess of relationships. With three little ones, John remarried. They had a son. Sparks began to fly.

Hanka, a feisty one, began to rebel. "She ain't tellin' me what to do."

The two girls landed at our place.

Pap wasn't with us anymore, but I had a job; two more places at the table posed no problem. That happened everywhere: Children becoming orphans. Working conditions were not of the safest. Many men were maimed or killed. The churches and the lodges got together and built an orphanage at Elmhurst, Pennsylvania. Hanka and Merka went to this orphanage. There was no other way.

Every year, as on a pilgrimage, Mama went to see the girls. Every month, I wrote them each a letter.

Again, came help. Ena's sister, Mary, came to America with a husband and two daughters. As soon as they were established, the girls went to live with her. Soon Hanka was old enough for a life of her own — able to work, take care of herself and her sister. She met a fine young man. Married. In due time, Merka also found a job, then married.

Today, they and their children live comfortably in the East.

Now we come to me.

After Pap died, I'll never know how Mama managed. Fortunately, we still had a few boarders: Uncle Mike's son and son-in-law and Gavaj were still with us. And I, at once, got a job in Squirrel Hill doing housework. The want-ad read, "Only a Slovak girl need apply," so I went.

And I really knew how to do the work: In the morning put the water on for coffee, then set the table. When the boss-lady awakened, take the baby. When the baby was asleep, I cleaned, I ironed, peeled potatoes, washed the dishes, ran to the store, minded the baby. All the things I did for Mama. Besides: They had a *library full of books*.

At first I only touched a few. Then I opened one. Then another. Soon I began to read. Then I heard the boss-lady: "HA-NI-KA," and I ran.

But every chance I got I sneaked back in; I had found the Children's Corner — found *The Swiss Family Robinson*, and didn't hear the boss-lady calling me.

When the second Sunday came, my Sunday off, she said not to come back anymore.

But I got another job working at Silianoff's Bakery in Wilmerding. Three dollars a week, and that was good. That's what girls got doing housework, and they had to work Sundays. Besides, Mr. Silianoff gave me bread. Sometimes a whole cake. And on Saturdays, cream puffs.

When school started, Mr. Silianoff told Mama that maybe I should go to school. Because I was good at numbers. He said I could work evenings and Saturdays. That's how I got to go to high school.

When I first entered high school — the exciting train ride to Braddock, the wide stairs to the upper floors, new books, a new teacher, a different room for every class, and I a part of it all, was almost more than I could stand.

But, by the time I got to the second year, the excitement was beginning to dissipate. Who cared about the Vicar of Wakefield, or the quality of mercy, when Eloise and Constance, in their nice dresses with shoes to match, did nothing but look at each other and giggle, and I, this already March, was still in galoshes because I was saving my shoes for Easter, but even in shoes, nobody would have noticed me anyhow. I had to get out of there, and I did.

"Mama," I asked, "could I wear my shoes before Easter? To look for a job," I added quickly.

"Okay," she said. "Maybe that will keep Aunt Julie's mouth shut."

"You think Annie will be a scribe someday," she mocked.

First I went to the telephone company where Elsie Simmons worked, but stammered at the interview. Then I went to the Westinghouse Airbrake in Wilmerding, but I was too small, so I went to the Westinghouse in East Pittsburgh to Clerical Employment where the Murray girls worked. I knew very well that our girls could never get work there, but our family name didn't sound Slovak. It sounded German.

Still nothing happened. April went by. May went by. Came June. Days were getting hot.

"All you're doing is wearing out your shoes," said Mama. I know it rankled that Little Julie and Little Liza both had jobs in restaurants. When I applied, the pile of pots in the kitchen sink was higher than I was.

"Don't worry," I replied. "I know I'll get a job." *If for no other reason, I thought, they'll get tired of seeing me every morning.*

Slowly, the truth began to dawn on me. Yes, when I filled out the application form I signed my name with confidence. It didn't have a foreign sound. "However, when I continued to where it said "nationality," I truthfully entered "Slovak." I couldn't lie. Now, what was I to do? Walk forever? That's when a thought occurred to me. I didn't have to lie. The next time a new girl appeared at the employment desk, I asked for a new application form. And in the space for nationality, I neatly wrote: "American."

In a few days I was asked, "How would you like to be a messenger girl?"

"A messenger! Oh, yes. I would love to be a messenger." I didn't know what that meant, but I knew I would love it.

After that came night school, followed by a job as a typist with a *desk and typewriter of my own.*

"Like in the funny papers? Like Tillie the Toiler? With a desk and typewriter?" Little Julie couldn't believe it either.

"Oh, yes," I gloated. "With a desk and typewriter all my own."

From typist I moved up to secretary, then to a private office of my own, then back to reality. I loved working with them, but never would I marry one of them. That's when I met John. He liked what he saw, I liked what I saw. Mary and Mikie were already working. Mama didn't need me anymore. We got married.

Now I'll do a fast-forward. The good times: one, two, three, four babies in a row. The bad times: layoffs, strikes and more strikes. All the while, John involved in politics: the telephone, day and night, ringing off the hook. Once a disgruntled voter complained to me, "When they run for office they promise you everything."

"Yes, lady," was my reply, "I know exactly what you mean. I'm still waiting for the things John promised me the day he asked to marry me."

Came a day I said, "Enough." I got out my Sears catalog, ordered a girdle, an up-lift, whipped myself into shape, went to Pitt, and got a position! With thirteen years of office experience I was literally snapped up. Like being blown into Heaven.

One by one, each of my children got to Pitt. As an evening student, John enrolled. I enrolled, my classes noon and evenings. My schedule: Mondays through Fridays belonged to Pitt. Saturdays, chores at home, and Sundays were for Mama.

By that time, my brothers and sisters were all on their own, two sisters out of state. Seeing that Mama went to a doctor, took her medicine, ate the right food, was left to me. My rightful job, I felt.

On Sundays, as we listened to Mass on the radio, as I cleaned and set to right the worn-out bed, the tired kitchen appliances, struggled with a sweeper that gasped for air, I vowed that AS SOON AS I GRADUATED, AS SOON AS I RECEIVED MY DIPLOMA, AS SOON AS I BEGAN TO MAKE A *LOT OF MONEY*, I WOULD FIX MAMA'S HOUSE FIT FOR A QUEEN.

Today I don't know where my diploma is. On the day I took my last exam, Mama died.

The reasons for my being at Pitt were now no more. The kids were graduated. They didn't need me anymore, and Mama didn't need me any more. So what did I do? I got a driver's license. I joined paint classes, poetry groups, did church work, volunteered at the local hospital.

Still, regularly, through all the years, I sat down to my beat-up Underwood for a little communion with the Past, each time capturing a little incident here, a little incident there. Now, at long last, the stories are on paper.

And Mama, I don't think you really wanted a house fit for a Queen; you were always happy with things as they were. On any Monday I can still see you: the clothes line already stretched, the water in the copper boiler already steaming, and you at the washboard:

> This is the way we wash our clothes,
> Wash our clothes,
> Wash our clothes.

> This is the way we wash our clothes,
> Every Monday morning.

Someday a time will come when we will not be a people of another land anymore; our faces will begin to resemble every other face. Smug with the new look, we will place our reliance on the banker, the warrior, and the silver-tongued orator. But something will be lacking. The new look will not become us.

That's when will emerge, on a Monday morning, a little gene. It will rise with the morning sun, build a new fire, draw fresh water, get out the washboard, and sing:

> This is the way we wash our clothes.

Epilogue – All Souls' Day

Now, on this All Souls' Day, I see and hear them all. They came to this country well-prepared for whatever was required of them. To work was to glorify God, a trait that came as naturally as breathing. The very name, Slav, derives from *Slava* (to praise), twin trait of "to serve."

First came the men. Unlettered and untried, over the Atlantic, *over the rainbow*, they came. What they found was prejudice.

This wasn't entirely new to them. If it had been otherwise, a free man in a free country, he wouldn't have known how to behave. The truth was, even though, in the course of civilized behavior, he had been released from serfdom, the serf in him never left. With a shrug of his shoulders, he did what already came naturally. He went to work.

Work was his forte, and jobs were everywhere: the steel mill, the railroad, the coal mine. Few, if any, planned on staying in this country. Work a few years, then back to *Stari Kraj*.

But America became addictive; many made more than one trip. Many stayed.

Women began to follow men, with one difference. Woman-wise, each brought with her a huge peasant bag from which she was never parted — not until she had reached her final destination.

Each bag, made of sturdy homespun, was stuffed with basics: towels, bed sheets, an embroidered tablecloth, at least one specially embroidered blouse and apron, and last but not least, a downy feather tick, the proud result of long winter nights of diligent plucking. It also represented the sum and total of her girlhood dreams.

Before long, there was a *Stari Kraj* in the new country — first in clusters, then in ghettos, then in villages. One man's success *became* two successes. Together, they more than survived; they became "rich."

I can still see them coming home from work, joshing one another, a spring in each step, the ones from the engine house so blackened that only the whites of their eyes showed. The large basin that hung on the outside wall of each house was for them, for washing down.

After stripping to the waist, after scrubbing down, after changing into a clean undershirt, into clean socks, after "Any mail today?" all retreated to the upstairs to wait for the call for supper.

The menu was identical in every household: every day except Friday and Sunday, beef soup with noodles. Sometimes *halushki*, or, if there was time, *pirohi*. Fridays: bean soup with noodles. Sundays were special. A huge pot of *holubki* (stuffed cabbage leaves; literally "little pigeons") with sauerkraut, breaded pork chops and during the winter months, *studzenina* (pig feet jelly).

Early Saturday morning the pig feet were charcoaled over hot coals, carefully nestled into a huge pot, blessed with a few cloves of plump garlic, covered with water, blessed again, then left to simmer all day on the back burner. When evening came it was strained and ladled into any and every odd bowl and dish we could find, then left on the pantry table to gel overnight.

Because of no refrigeration, there was a second delivery on Saturday. All Sunday cooking was finished by midnight Saturday. Sunday was: church in the morning, home to eat, afternoons visiting. Evenings, after supper, there was talk and music and storytelling — always the Old Country, and always, "Someday we'll all be back home again."

Then came the Big War, WWI, and that did it. The separation of the old from the new began. Roots began to take hold. The children, already enrolled into school, came home with a new language, new ways.

Death also played its role: A little grave tied a family to the new land as nothing else could. A family could pick up and leave, but how can one leave a little grave?

And staying, they prospered. A glow of pride began to show. "Look, my hands. The hands of a working man still, but my Jozef? A white shirt he wear to work." The shrug on his shoulder began to look suspiciously like a chip.

Still, the ache and longing for the Old Country never totally went away, even to the third and fourth generations.

Some married "outsiders," ashamed of their background, of the small beginnings, of crude Old Country ways. But the Past will never go away. It will live forever in the rhythmic sound of the sledge hammer that drove the spike that held the rail that controlled the freight that went to all points of the globe; in the rhythmic motion of Mama's arm that cut the noodles that went into the soup that fed the men after a hard day at the mill or on the railroad tracks.

•   •   •

The Mass was now coming to an end. I glanced at Mrs. Donelko clutching her rosary, head nodding in pious supplication. Her heavenly confidante? Not the Almighty. Her peasant soul wouldn't dare. His mother. She would intercede.

-"Hanicka," she had cried to me at the curbstone, as if I were still skipping along the sidewalks, still running into her kitchen to borrow something.

The cantor was now intoning the final "Amen" of the Mass proper, Father Anselm was descending to the Tetrapod.

An Aside:

The tetrapod is a small table down from the altar that holds the icon of the day. It is also a stopping point for any worshipper who feels the need to come closer to the altar, closer to God, so to speak, to genuflect, always done with style.

A beautifully executed genuflection could stop the most ardent of prayers in mid-air. Beginning with the closure of the first three fingers of the right hand, forming a trinity, the fingers touch the lips. Eyes and head turn heavenward, the arm begins to rise, continues with a sweeping motion toward the altar. A slight pause.

The body bends slowly downward until the three fingers touch the floor. A pause. The movement is then reversed: head begins to rise, arm toward the altar, the body straightens, the fingers touch the lips. The arc is completed.

Then two more times. Three in all. The performance, admittedly a bit on the showy side, is amply redeemed by the courage it took.

Now Father Anselm, with a list of names of the departed, is himself standing at the tetrapod. Beginning with the first letter of the alphabet, he begins to intone, a few at a time, the names of the deceased. The cantor, in perfect counterpoint, matching his rhythm to that of the priest, chants the triple "God have mercy, God have mercy, God have mercy."

In mesmeric cadence, the reading of the names continues: from priest to cantor, from cantor to priest, the tones overlapping almost as if a soul would fall through the cracks if this weren't so — from priest to cantor, then wafted onward into the open arms of eternity, and when the last name was chanted, before the opening closed, I followed.

I am running toward Pap. He is reaching out to me. "Don't cry. Don't cry."

I am outside playing. "Run, sheep, run."

It's getting dark, and the mothers are beginning to call. But I don't want to go. Not yet. "Please, God, just one more minute, to run, to play."

I see Susie. "Don't go, Susie, don't go."

I am running again, backward, backward, then forward to another beginning. *The earth is without form, void, and darkness is upon the face of the deep*, and I am there.

God is saying, "*Let there be light*," and I am crying, "Please, for me . . . ."

And He, "*For everything there is a season, a time to mourn, and a time to sing.*"

"I know, I know, but for me, once more, that fragment of Time that was mine: a planet that knew both sun and rain, a house that knew both laughter and tears. Let me remember forever, the time that gave me Pap and Mama, the boarders, my brothers and sisters, running to Aunt Julie's. "An egg. Mama needs an egg. To Aunt Liza's. A cup of sugar. The Murrays, the Donelkos, and Susie — Susie for whom all Creation cried. And that's when it happened. As it always did. Every time I came to the best part of a story, a call from Mama, "ANNIE." And now, again.

"ANNIE!" came a voice. It was Him. I recognized the tone. I was being scolded again. Like the time He said, because I had been grumbling, "I gave you a car, didn't I?" Now, again.

"What's your hurry, Annie? Haven't I told you: For everything there is a time? But you can't wait.

"I am with you always. When your eyes went bad, mine did, too. We began to see things others didn't. When you began to stammer, I did, too. Together, we learned to listen.

"And you sang: from morning until night. When time came to do the dishes, it was either a two-verse pile or a twelve-verse pile, and if any dishes were left over, you sang an extra verse, and if there was some song left over, you looked around for something else to wash, and all of Heaven smiled.

"You were given feet for running — for dancing. Don't you think I, too, got a chuckle when, at only three, you danced on a tavern bar at the Wall Hotel? And I agreed with your Uncle Fedor for stopping the hoochy koochy. Although it wasn't your fault. It was his for bringing home that Kewpie doll, then showing you how to wind it up.

"When you cry, I cry. When you sing, I sing. When you die, I die. Together, we rise again. But, Annie, you just can't wait for the next chapter.

"There is an order that must be observed: for everything a time. But you can't wait. You think that all I do is sit up here on a cloud making rules? Annie, I am not the Lord of the Universe. I AM THE UNIVERSE, and you are a part of it, together with Me: of Each Other, by Each Other, and for Each Other.

"Back up, Annie. Back up. There are things you have yet to do. Come to think of it, on this very All Souls' Day, there is somebody you forgot."

I did? I blinked my eyes and He was gone. But He was right. All during Mass something had been nudging at me. I looked around. Nothing amiss. No one was even aware I had been to eternity and back.

Father Anselm was returning to the altar. Everybody began to rise. Facing the people, he introduced the final chant, *"Vicnaja Pamjat,"* a chant so achingly beautiful I felt my soul beginning to soar again. *Who was it I had forgotten?*

The service was now over. Father Anselm was leaving the altar, the people were beginning to shuffle out of church, the rosary ladies back on their knees for a few more prayers that may have been forgotten. The altar boys were snuffing out the candles. Left were the candles still flickering on the votive stands. *Resisting the call to go back,* I thought.

My eyes centered on the block of candles I had lit for our boarders. What, or who, had I forgotten? I rose in my pew. Began to move forward. I began to hear them.

Pap and Mama are in the kitchen putting the lunch buckets together, Uncle Fedor already there, the men still upstairs grumbling their prayers.

Soon all the men were in the kitchen. That's when I heard, still upstairs, *Uncle George!*

Uncle George, I forgot. I didn't even light a candle for you. But I can do it now. This one. Near the men. I applied a taper. Quickly, the light flared, rose, and stayed.

But Uncle George, I said in self-defense, *it's not entirely my fault. You never did do things properly, in the prescribed way—always coming to our house when everything was eaten and everybody in bed.* Because you were out of a job, I know. I used to hear Pap scold you.

But when morning came, after all the men had gone downstairs, I heard you pray—first for your wife and children, then for all of us, then for yourself: "And for me, a little glass of bourbonette." I heard you.

Then you didn't come any more. Pap inquired everywhere. Out there chasing the American dream, you were. Did you find it?

But you never worried. As you said to Aunt Julie one day when she warned you, "Who will bury you when you die?" you replied, "No worry. In America, nobody is left above ground."

Wherever he is, America, be kind to him.

As for now, because for you there was no *"Vicnaja Pamjat,"* we'll do it your way: A little glass of bourbonette.

LEST WE FORGET:
A FEW PAGES OF RECIPES

Aunt Annie, why don't you write a recipe book?"

A recipe book? I just finished a book. But he doesn't know.

That was Tommy, grandson of a long ago cousin. Retired now, he became one of a group of retirees who get together once a month at the church to make *pirohi* (picrogi).

Because of his nice height, he had been delegated for kitchen duty, to stand over huge pots of boiling water. He had just stepped out for a bit of air to where I was working.

I'll admit to being flattered by his attention — a little old lady at the rolling machine — but a book? I'd need another lifetime.

Tommy read the look on my face. "I mean it, Aunt Annie. All those good things my mother used to make — sweet-sour potato with green bean soup. Nobody makes that stuff anymore."

I agreed with him. Nobody makes that stuff anymore. I also agreed that his idea was a good one, but...

"All those soups," he continued. "Monday, Tuesday, Wednesday and Thursday, beef with noodles, then on Friday, because of no meat, something different. I ate more on Friday than I did during the week."

"Same here. I could hardly wait for Friday to come. Remember beans and *lechki* (noodle flakes)? I could never eat enough."

"And *rosol* (sauerkraut) soup."

"But noodles had to be *tarhani* (torn) for that soup. No other kind would do."

"Then lentil soup, with oyster crackers."

"Or split pea soup with carrots. All that was needed was a good *zaprashka* (a roux)."

We both stopped to savor the old taste.

"Remember the farmer-lady who came once a month, always on a Friday, with buttermilk; thick curds with flecks of butter still floating through it. For that we had to peel a peck of potatoes, and while they were cooking, mother put a huge scoot of butter into the skillet to brown, into which was added a generous amount of chopped onions.

When the potatoes were cooked and mashed, the butter and onions were mixed into the pot. Raw butter would never do. Everyone got a bowl of potatoes, another bowl with buttermilk, and that is how we ate it; a spoonful of potato dipped into the buttermilk had a taste like no other.

"I worked with a Greek girl once who told me they ate the same thing with this difference: each person was served a mound of potatoes, around which buttermilk was poured. Like an island.

"Even the Irish ate potatoes. 'Irish potatoes,' they were called. Do you remember that? White potatoes were once called 'Irish potatoes' as opposed to sweet potatoes?"

We still ate our share, and more. If any were left over, my mother made *loksha* (a crepe). After dishes were done, we stood in line for those.

"And we stood in line for pork drippings. On the day Mama made roasted pork pieces, when dishes were done, there was still this pan of pork drippings in the oven. Mother brought it to the table, filled a bowl with broken pieces of bread and got out the mustard. We stood in line, picked up a piece of bread, dipped it into the pan and spread the bread with mustard. That was better than the supper."

"And when Lent came, so many kinds of *halushki* (a pasta); *tarhani* (torn), *rezanki* (cut), *trepani* (dumplings), some with sautéed sauerkraut, and sometimes with cottage cheese."

"And *trepani halushki* (potato dumplings)."

"Oh, yes. Tricky to make but more than worth the effort. My sister Mary's husband Mike was an expert. Because his mother had been bedridden for so long, he had to learn to cook, and potato dumplings were his supreme achievement. To fun-loving Mary, the making to them was a bother, which is why when the yen wouldn't be denied, Mike took over the kitchen. The ritual began with two grated potatoes, one egg, and flour to the right consistency.

"If a small amount dropped into a pot of boiling water falls apart, all that is needed is more flour. When a dumpling holds together, the process may begin.

"The total mixture is piled onto a flat dish. With a soup spoon, a controlled amount is smoothed over toward the edge of the dish, then with the tip of the spoon the dumpling begins, the smaller (the size of a bean) the better. Working fast, this doesn't take too long. When my mother made them, there was a houseful of boarders. My father helped — he on one side, and she on the other.

"When the dumplings are all in the pot, they are stirred with a wooden spoon until they begin to rise to the top, then let to simmer for about two minutes, drained, then mixed with whatever filling had been prepared. Mike's favorite was cottage cheese.

"Having quickly drained his dumplings (lest they cook too much), he reached for the skillet where the cottage cheese and butter and onions were on warm, mixed the two together, scooped a generous portion onto a plate, stepped over to the table, sat down, and like a *pan* (a lord) began to eat. And nobody bothered him. Not until he had finished and picked up his lunch bucket (he worked the second shift), did the others scramble for what was left. And he always made enough."

We, Tommy and I, held a moment of silence over that one, then he said, "Remember the cornmeal mush ... slow-cooked, poured into a mold to set, then sliced and sautéed in butter."

"And another thing. We didn't know about french toast, but we had something just as good, maybe better. Sometimes, when my mother had the time, she would brown some butter in a skillet, toss in broken pieces of bread, stir them around a bit, cracked in a few eggs, scramble everything together, and that's what we had for breakfast. No french toast could possibly taste as good."

"Does anyone make that anymore?"

"No, not anymore. But, Tommy, there is a good reason for that. We were laughed at, even about the kind of food we ate. Italian spaghetti fared better than our halushki. We began to switch, began to mention foods like casseroles, marmalades, and fillet mignons. We wanted to be Americans."

"I guess," said Tommy. "But I sure miss the old stuff."

What else could I say? I looked at Tommy, and he looked back at me, sadness in both our eyes. There was nothing more to say.

"Tommy," I heard myself saying, "We'll do it. And we don't need a book. All we need is a chapterful of a few good pages."

* * *

Beginning with soups, I will start with number one, the one made every Monday, Tuesday, Wednesday, and Thursday: beef and noodles. Quantities of the recipes will be for four servings.

Beef and Noodle Soup

Not everybody could afford a nice chunk of beef. Some couldn't even afford the plate boil. Soup bones had to do.

1 LB of plate boil (a bone with little meat on it)
1 nice soup bone, cracked
1 medium can of tomatoes
Enough water to cover it

Simmer for one hour. Then add:

2 or 3 medium-sized potatoes
2 or 3 medium-sized carrots
1 medium onion
2 stalks of celery
About 4 sprigs of parsley, depending on size
1 good sized cabbage core (saved from making stuffed cabbage rolls) or a wedge of cabbage.
Salt and pepper.

Simmer for another hour. When done, strain. Pick the meat off the plate. Sometimes, a kind butcher left some meat on the soup bone. Toss the meat into the soup. The onion and celery goes back into the soup. The parsley is tossed out. Potatoes and carrots go back into the soup.

When ready to serve, lift our the potatoes and carrots. Sometimes these are served separately, or mashed together with butter, and because this combination was so good, sometime another potato and carrot was added to the pot. If there was a chunk of beef in the pot, it was sidled in beside the potatoes and carrots.

The soup was served, of course, with a generous scoop of noodles.

Because most of the recipes for soup require a *zaprashka* (a roux), I will begin here with a good roux. This may be divided in half.

Zaprashka (a roux)

1 stick of butter
⅓ to ½ cup of flour
2 medium onions, chopped

Sautee butter until it begins to turn brown. Stir in the flour, add the onions, cook over low to medium heat, stirring now and then until nice brown. Set aside. When cooled, dilute with ½ cup of water.

The following soup is Tommy's favorite... and at our house.

Sweet Sour Potato and Green Bean Soup

4 to 6 medium potatoes
4 cups of green beans
¼ cup of vinegar
¼ cup of sugar

Cover with water. Simmer until cooked. Add the diluted roux. Bring to boiling point. Boil one minute. Then add:

½ cup evaporated milk

For a rich soup, add the full can of milk. More water if too thick.

The next soup, like most of the others, provides an acceptable soup for Good Friday: a no-meat no-dairy products strict fast day. Because margarine is a vegetable shortening, the roux is made with margarine. The milk, of course, is left out. Oyster crackers are permitted.

Lentil Soup

Most brands of lentils include directions for cooking soup. Follow the directions on package. While lentils are cooking, sautee in a skillet ½ stick of butter until light brown. Add 1 or 2 chopped onions, reduce heat to low, and continue cooking until a light brown. When lentils are cooked, add the butter and onions. Canned, evaporated milk may or may not be added.

Split Pea Soup

Same as lentil soup.

To both these soups, people have begun to add carrots, celery, parsley ... even potatoes, but this wasn't done in the early days. There was never anything left over. Perhaps this is why today's soup has a different taste. Like everything else, once something different is added, the original "taste" is gone.

Beans and Lechki (noodle flakes)

The bean here is the pinto bean. Not the cranberry, and not the kidney. Sometimes this soup is made with navy beans. This is nice for a change. The lechki is a noodle cut into tiny squares. These may be purchased in the stores.

1 package of beans (16 oz)
1 package of lechki
1 recipe of roux

Sort and rinse beans. Soak for about 6 hours. Do not throw away the soak water as directed on the package. Much of the bean flavor is already in the water. Add more water to cover beans, simmer until done. Add the roux. Bring to a boil. Keep the cooked lechki separate. Combine when ready to eat. When I make this soup, before adding the roux, I mash the beans a little. We like the soup that way.

Now here is a must: rosol soup. Rosol is sauerkraut juice. When making sauerkraut and pork, or sautéed sauerkraut with halushki, or for anything, I squeeze out the juice and save it for the rosol soup. Sometimes I can't wait that long, so I just chop up about a cup or two of sauerkraut, add enough water to make two quarts, cook for about half an hour, add the full recipe of roux, and there it is. But, without the tarhani noodles, this soup is not right.

But, when making pirohi, there may be some dough left over. I make sure to have extra dough. When the pirohi are done, I roll this extra dough very thin, then lay it on a cloth somewhere to dry. This may take until the next day. When dried, just break into small pieces. These noodles are not quite as good as when torn into boiling water, but good enough to satisfy a sudden craving.

Another important version of the rosol soup is it provides the basis for a very important soup served on Christmas Eve.

Mushroom Soup

Dried mushrooms (fresh aren't the same) are soaked overnight. To these is added sauerkraut and the juice. When cooked, all you need is the roux. Bring to a boil. One has to wait until Christmas Eve for this one.

Pirohi (Pierogi)

2 cups flour
2 eggs
2 tablespoons oil
½ teaspoon salt
Warm water
Butter

Mix flour, eggs, oil and salt. Add enough water to make a medium (does not stick to hands) dough. Knead well. Divide into two portions.

Roll one part thin. Cut into circles. Place desired filling into center of each circle. Fold one side to touch the other side, making a semi-circle and making sure the filling does not touch the edges. Gently press the edges together, then pinch firmly so it will hold when dropped into boiling water. Repeat with second half of dough.

To cook, drop into boiling water. When pirohi rise to the top, cook for about two more minutes. Drain. Pour over with browned butter.

FILLINGS: (these should be made first)

1. Potato filling   2 large potatoes, cooked and mashed.
½ teaspoon of salt.
Shredded mild yellow cheese.

2. Sauerkraut filling   Drain the sauerkraut. You may wash the kraut or not. I don't. But save the juice (the *rosol*) for rosol soup. Chop up the kraut, throw a cupful into the juice jar for the soup, sautee in rest of skillet with butter and onions until beginning to brown.

3. Cabbage filling   Chop fine one small head of cabbage, sautee with butter and onions until beginning to brown. Add a little salt.

4. Lekvar filling   This one is tricky. Sometimes the lekvar is too soft. However, two tablespoons of tapioca in the mix a day ahead will remedy this.

Pirohi are best when first cooked, however, they do freeze well. To restore there are two ways: one, sautee until brown on both sides, then serve with sour cream. Second, you can sautee the butter with a generous amount of chopped onions. When almost done, lay the piro-hi over the onions.

Now come the dough recipes. Most of these have already been picked up in the Pittsburgh area by other peoples, and are easy to make.

Halushki: a pasta. A generic term that can apply to a dough that is cut, or torn, or made into dumplings. In Pittsburgh, *halushki* means a wide dough, cooked, then combined with sautéed cabbage. The native term for this is *rezanki* (cut noodles), and these are served with sautéed cabbage, or sautéed sauerkraut or cottage cheese. I will give all versions under the term *halushki*.

Buy (you don't have to make these) a package of noodles. Look for a noodle about ⅓" wide. If crinkled, the better. If the noodle comes in long pieces, these will have to be broken. Some are already small.

Cook as directed. Combine with filling. Serve.

FILLINGS:

1. Sauerkraut.   Squeeze out the juice (which you will save of course) chop up, sautee slowly in browned butter and onions.

2. Cabbage.   A favorite in these parts. Chop up a small head of cabbage. Sautee in browned butter and onions. About ½ hour or more.

3. Cottage cheese.   This is a little tricky. The proper cheese is the dry cottage cheese. But some prefer the cream cheese. I sometimes combine the two.

Whereas the cabbage and the sauerkraut are cooked together with the butter and onions and are easier to handle, if too much heat is applied to cottage cheese it's ruined. And putting cold cottage cheese into the noodles makes the whole thing cold.

What I do is first sautee the butter with the onions. I turn off the heat, and when the skillet is cooled off enough I dump in the cottage cheese and stir to mix with the butter and onions that are still hot enough to warm up the cottage cheese. The cottage cheese, by the way, should be at room temperature.

Holubki, I believe, are here to stay. Unhappily, the original version seems to have disappeared. So, I am including three versions: the old way, the new way, and a new version of the new version: my own invention.

Holubki (stuffed cabbage rolls)
literally translated, **holubki** means pigeons or doves

1 LB ground meat
1 medium cabbage
½ to ⅓ up long grain rice
1 medium onion, sautéed in
Bacon fat
Salt and pepper

There are many ways of making these. I will give two, the old way without the tomato (the tomato at one time was considered a Love Apple and used for display only). All methods begin with separating the leaves from the cabbage head. I do mine by immersing the whole head into boiling water, then with a sharp knife and a fork begin separating the leaves. Some claim that putting the cabbage head into the microwave will do the job.

After the leaves have been loosened and have had a chance to cool, trim away the spine.

The old method was this: In 1 cup of water, parboil the rice. Bring water and rice to a full boil, then turn off heat. Do not cook the rice.

Next, in a skillet, sautee the onions in the bacon fat until onion is limp. Add the ground meat. Stir. When meat loses its pink color it is done. Drain rice, add to meat. Begin wrapping.

Place a tablespoonful or more of the meat into the center of a leaf. Begin wrapping up from the bottom, over from the left, over from the right, down from the top, and then lay gently into a baking pan. This method is for sale, or for home consumption. For a wedding, the Canadian women have come up with a new and easier way. They cut the leaf into fourths, place a small portion of the meat mix into the center, and just roll up. No tucking in, right, then left. But, then, they don't have a "pigeon" anymore. What they have is a "sardine." These were layered with sauerkraut. They are excellent without.

The "new" method has a few significant alterations. Added to the ingredients is garlic, tomato sauce, and ketchup.

Sautéed onion and garlic is added to the raw meat and the raw rice. Add ¼ cup or more of ketchup. Proceed with the rolls as directed. Pour 26 ounces of tomato sauce over them, diluted with ¼ to ½ cup of water. Proceed as directed. Now comes my own and my best invention.

Sweet and Sour Holubki

To the sauce, add ¼ cup of brown sugar and ¼ cup of vinegar.

Losksha (a potato crepe)

Left over potatoes
An equal amount of flour
One stick of butter
A hot heavy skillet

These used to be rolled out as round as a dish pan then baked on the bottom of a coal stove oven, but we don't have coal stoves anymore. I now bake smaller crepes that fit into a top stove skillet.

Combine the potatoes with the flour ... the amount of flour depends on how soft or hard the potatoes are. Divide the mix into balls somewhat larger than a walnut.

Working one ball at a time, flatten with floured hands, place on a well-floured cloth or board, flour the top of the ball, cover with waxed paper, and roll into a thin crepe, turning over once, making sure there is enough flour on both sides. Otherwise, the dough will stick and will have to be discarded.

Run a stick of butter over the hot skillet and gently lay the crepe onto the skillet. It will brown in blisters after about a minute. Flip over, run the butter over the top baked side.

When bottom is browned, flip the crepe onto a platter, quickly roll up and hand to first person in line, or place on a platter until all are done. These warm up nicely in a microwave.

One can become quite adept at this ... when the first crepe begins to brown, there is time to begin rolling the next one. With a lineup waiting, this is fun.

Slatka's Kvasnu Kapusta (Sweet and sour cabbage)

A truly pleasant dish. First I would like to explain something: why do we say "sweet cabbage?" Is there any other kind? It's a quirk in translation. In the Slavic tongue, there is no sauerkraut. The term is "sour cabbage." That is the reason for the term "sweet cabbage." But I like it that way; it kind of acknowledges from whence we came. Now, the recipe (of course, we used leftovers).

1 package of sauerkraut, chopped up
1 medium-sized head of cabbage, chopped up
Water to cover
A roux

Cook the cabbage and the sauerkraut until done. About a half hour. Stir in the prepared (diluted) roux. Bring to a boil. In the early days, the pot was set at the back of stove where the *kapusta* was kept warm all day. Served over mashed potatoes, this is good eating. Anytime.

Kminkova Polivka
(Caraway Seed Soup, aka Egg Dumpling Soup)

This soup, once, was given only to women who had just given birth, and to persons who were ill. Children learned to pretend an illness, especially in the case where one sibling became sick. Usually, the whole family "coincidentally" became sick.

Then along came a wiseacre who said, "if the soup can make a sick person well, then the same soup can prevent a well person from becoming ill."

4 eggs, beaten
Flour to make a dough... just enough to hold it together
Caraway seeds
A roux

Make the dough. Go easy. It's easier to add flour than take it away. When a bit dropped into boiling water holds its shape, it is right. Continue with the rest of the dough. Add a tablespoon of caraway seeds. Salt and pepper. Cook gently until dumplings begin to rise to the top. Lower heat. Continue cooking for a minute or so, then lower the heat. Cover the pot for about ten minutes. The dumplings will puff up. Add the roux. Bring slowly to a boil.

I make this often, especially if my meals have not been up to par. It makes meal-making well again. The next recipe is also an effective meal saver.

Potato Pancakes

4 potatoes, peeled and grated
1 onion grated.
1 teaspoon salt
½ teaspoon pepper
1 egg beaten
2 or a little more tablespoons of flour. Be careful with the flour. A little too much will ruin the whole thing.

Mix all ingredients. Put a little shortening into a skillet. When hot, drop the potato mixture in 2 or 3 tablespoon sizes. If the edges are lacy, the pancake should be a good one. Brown on both sides, then lay on paper towel to absorb the fat.

Serve with applesauce.

Because of the nice things that used to made with bread dough, I will include a few recipes.

First of all, on the day my mother made bread (huge loaves that took forever to cool) she made a flat bread for that day's supper. When slathered with butter, there was never enough.

Bobalky

These bits of dough (about the size of a small walnut when raised) are beginning to appear in the local supermarkets, and I am wondering, do other people know what to do with them? This is how they are made.

Begin with about one pound of dough. Divide into fist-size pieces. Hand roll on a floured board to ½" in diameter. Cut into small pieces. Toss with flour. Place the pieces onto a greased cookie sheet. Let rise for about 10 minutes. Bake in a medium oven until light brown.

Have filling ready: sweet cabbage, sauerkraut, or cottage cheese. When ready to serve, pour boiling water over the bobalky to just soften. Do not turn them into mush. Drain quickly, add filling, and serve.

A filling reserved for holidays is one made of poppyseeds.

Poppyseed filling: Cook 1-1½ cups of ground poppyseed in ¾ cups of water for 10 minutes. Boil three cups of milk, add 1 cup of sugar, according to taste, and pour over the poppyseed mix. Add to bobalky.

Bobalky, by the way, were served only at Christmas Eve... a tradition we still uphold in our family.

Another item made form bread dough and served only on feast days is the pagach. Any of the aforementioned fillings may be used as directed, with the exception of the cottage cheese. Add enough sugar to dry cottage to be able to taste. No poppyseed for pagach.

For pagach, about 1½ pounds was saved from the dough. Because the holiday bread was richer than every day bread, i.e. more butter and more sugar, it was perfect for the pagach.

We are using already kneaded and raised dough, of course. Divide dough into three or four portions. Let rise, covered, for ten minutes to rest.

Take one piece at a time, flatten with the back of the hand. Place filling in center and draw up and pinch edges together. Cover and let rise for another ten minutes.

Turn dough over onto a floured board, and press very carefully with the back of the hand all around, then, with rolling pin, roll out slowly, being careful that the filling not break through to 10 to 12 inches in diameter. Place carefully onto a baking sheet. Bake in medium oven until nicely brown. When done, brush with butter.

One more thing; when baking with dry cottage cheese, mix 1 egg yolk to every ½ cup used. Don't forget the sugar. A pagach could also be made with pierogi potato filling.

Someone said once "Mankind's best and nicest invention is still the art of cookery." If only someone would invent an easy way of cleaning up a kitchen.